THE RELIGIOUS EXPERIENCE
OF JESUS
AND HIS DISCIPLES

Religious Experience Series

Edward J. Malatesta, S.J., General Editor

Religious Experience Series
Volume 9

The Religious Experience of Jesus

and His Disciples

by
Jacques Guillet, S.J.

Translated by
Sister Mary Innocentia Richards, S.N.J.M.

ABBEY PRESS
St. Meinrad, Indiana 47577
1975

The present work is a translation of the article "Jésus," which first appeared in the *Dictionnaire de Spiritualité,* Paris, Beauchesne, 1973, vol. 8, cols. 1065-1109.

© 1975 by Edward J. Malatesta, S.J.
Library of Congress Catalog Card Number: 75-210
ISBN: 0-87029-044-4
Printed in the United States of America

Preface

This study presents a number of special problems. In order to show the place Jesus holds in Christian life and in the history of Christian spirituality, one would need a complete dictionary. The specific objective of the *Dictionary of Spirituality* is to define and describe the varying forms of man's relationship with Jesus. Justifiably, the *Dictionary* could be a single work with the title *Jesus*. There can be no question here of handling the subject according to what is said in the entire New Testament or even in any one of the Gospels. The author of the article "John the Evangelist" could only speak of the spiritual doctrine of John in the context of a lengthy discussion of the life and personality of Jesus.[1] What, then, can be done in the short space reserved for this article on Jesus?

Perhaps His spiritual life could be studied. We might attempt to grasp and to explain what His experience of God was and the way in which this experience was manifest in His life, in His reactions to men and events. However, we shall see that the essential quality of this experience is its intangibility; it defies description. Accordingly, many of our contemporaries hold the opinion that this article is decidedly one that must not be written. If it is perfectly legitimate to present the message of Jesus, to try to describe His actions and their effects, it is useless and dangerous to aim at depicting His personality and His reactions to events.

But that is exactly what this study proposes to achieve. What is the meaning of the lived "spiritual" experience of Jesus for the Christian? What possibility have we of discovering it? What is the relationship of the lived experience of Jesus to that of the Christian?

Abbreviations

DS	*Dictionnaire de Spiritualité*	Paris
TDNT	Theological Dictionary of the New Testament	Grand Rapids

Contents

Chapter I

The Acts of the Apostles

Although the Acts are among the latest writings of the New Testament, thanks to the discourses of the early chapters they permit us to go back to a very ancient period, perhaps the oldest that can be known, regarding Christian self-awareness and experience. Although the discourses cannot be considered reproductions of ancient documents, since, in all probability, they were composed by St. Luke, the author of the Acts, numerous features, particularly the archaic nature of the affirmations of faith and the names given to Jesus, show that Luke had access to ancient traditions and that he wished to retain something of their originality.

A. Discourses

In all the discourses the manner of presenting Jesus and the attitude to be taken in relation to Him are so similar that it is impossible not to see in them a schema of basic development in which the initial form of the Gospel appears as the message of the primitive Church. According to this schema, the relationship between the Christian experience and that of Jesus appears at first sight very tenuous. All these discourses have but one end in view, conversion; and this conversion is linked not so much with what Jesus experienced in His mortal life, but rather with what God and men did in the circumstances of His death and resurrection. ". . . Jesus of Nazareth, a man attested to you by God . . . you crucified and killed by the hands of lawless men. This Jesus God raised up. . . . God has made Him both Lord and Christ. . . . Repent, and be bap-

tized every one of you in the name of Jesus Christ for the forgiveness of your sins; and you shall receive the gift of the Holy
Spirit" (Acts 2:22-38; see also 3:13-26; 4:10-12; 5:30-31;
10:37-43; 13:26-39). The situations are different. At
Jerusalem, Peter confronts the very audience that has heard
Jesus and rejected Him, the anonymous crowd of the city, the
frequenters of the Temple, the prominent members of the
Sanhedrin; at Caesarea in Palestine, a group of pagans sym-
pathetic toward Judaism; at Antioch in Pisidia, the congrega-
tion in a synagogue on the sabbath day. Everywhere the message is the same: a call to conversion and the certainty of ob-
taining pardon for sins and a new life, the life which God expects of men and which is possible because of Jesus.

Jesus holds a prominent place in all these discourses, and
this is brought out by the form of the sentence that almost
always begins by placing first His name and then His life experiences. It is worthy of note, however, that between the
events of His life and the awaited conversion of the hearers
the relationship is more one of cause and effect than one of
continuity.

The possibility of God's pardon is now proclaimed to all
men because Jesus died and rose again and because, rejected
by men, He has been glorified by God. As for the hearers in
Jerusalem, those far or near who by their actions, their com-
plicity, or simply by their silence are responsible for the death
of Jesus, there is this logical conclusion: these men participated
in a monstrous crime that touched God directly. From this
sin God draws a most surprising victory. He brings back to
life His envoy and pardons the guilty ones. How does it
happen that this pardon includes all men, howsoever un-
acquainted they may have been with this drama? Jewish faith
supplies the answer. This man was the Messiah, the one given
by God to His people in order to open a new era, not only
for the children of Israel, but for the whole human race.

Thus the oldest examples of preaching in the Church seem
to indicate that what is essential to faith resides in a fundamental relationship with Jesus, but not as though this relationship establishes a parallel between the lived experience of
Jesus and the experience of the Christian convert. Indubitably,
if Jesus is the Messiah, a unique experience must be implied.

However, there is no attempt to recover that experience and still less to make of it the prototype of Christian experience. Because He was the Messiah given by God, every man is called to believe in Him to find the salvation of God. The link is essential; it is transmitted simultaneously through the person and the event, in other words by a certain event experienced by a person which begins a new relationship between God and man. In this relationship Jesus holds a place no other could hold. It is He who cements anew the broken bond between man and God, the bond of reconciliation between God and sinners, the immediate communication between God and the human race. That this is the vision that results spontaneously from the text of the discourses cannot be doubted. It is invaluable because it is basically Christian; and this is due to the place accorded to Christ and is typically Jewish because it leaves the whole initiative and sovereignty to God. Is it necessary to conclude that here we find Christianity in a pure state, shorn of later additions, those of dubious mysticism and of a myth-making dogmatism?

However valuable and authentic this first form of Christian faith may be, it is, nevertheless, as far back as its earliest expression, richer and more expressive than is evident from the description we have just given. It is not content to have Jesus play the major role of Messiah. It sets up a series of relationships between Jesus and God, between Jesus and men, prior to or after the crucial event of His death and resurrection.

The Jesus described in these discourses is truly at every moment of His life recognizable by His relationships and by His way of living for others. All the discourses are built up in three steps: life on earth, death and resurrection, and the action of the risen Jesus. In each of the three steps, different yet converging elements appear. In the first, Jesus is characterized by His manner of acting. He performs miracles— ". . . with mighty works and wonders and signs which God did through Him in your midst" (Acts 2:22); ". . . He went about doing good and healing" (10:38); ". . . they could charge Him with nothing deserving death" (13:28);—and this unique combination of power and goodness is a sign that God is with Him, that He is the "Holy and Righteous One," "the Author of life" (2:22; 3:14; 10:38). God acts in Jesus, making Him the bearer of His power and generosity toward men. In the second stage the unique rapport between God and Jesus appears. This rapport is expressed by words and varying titles borrowed from Israel's expressions of expectation in the Old Testament: "Holy One" (2:27; 3:14; 4:27; 13:35), "Holy Servant" (2:27; 4:27), "Christ" (3:18), "Son" 13:33). Here a detail strikes us, the use of the possessive form: "your Holy One," "your Servant," "His Messiah," "my Son." This possessive form is normally not used in the preceding stage or in the following one. At the very time when Jesus is rejected by men and delivered up to death, this mysterious component appears, this expression of the bond that death cannot destroy and that explains the resurrection. Because Jesus comes from God alone, because He accomplishes to the very end His God-given mission, His role is defined as He is given up to His frightful destiny and exalted to an unparalleled position. In the third stage Jesus seems to possess a divine grandeur and to be endowed with a new power that puts Him in relationship with every creature. At this point we note new titles: "Lord" (2:36; 10:36), "Judge of the living and the dead" (10:42), "Savior" (5:31; 13:23). These titles do not signify simply an unequaled greatness and divine stature; they simultaneously proclaim the extension of this powerful generosity and beneficence to the whole world, the same characteristics portrayed during His earthly life. The risen Jesus is both glorified as God and given by God to the world as its Savior (3:20; 4:12; 10:43; 13:38).

Taken singly, these annotations may seem of slight value, but their convergence gives them great importance. Although we cannot say that Luke used a planned and systematic pattern of speech, we must note that the words, the traditional titles used to describe the actions and destiny of Jesus, take on varying and definite coloring according to the stages of His life. The Jesus who goes about in the Jewish fatherland, who dies abandoned by men and "exalted at the right hand of God" (2:33), who receives all power over the living and the dead is indeed not only the same Jesus, living a unique destiny: He is constantly, in different ways, in connection and in communication with God and men, with all those whom

He met in His lifetime, with all men after His resurrection. At this stage of the Gospel, as it emerges in the Acts, one cannot yet speak of an experience of Jesus that may be described. Nevertheless, it is already clear that it is not a matter of a simple event. There is a profound harmony between the person and the event. If Jesus' life and death have meaning for all men, it is not simply because God has so decided. It is because Jesus by all that He was and all that He experienced called, so to speak, for this universal fellowship with all humanity.

B. Witnesses to Jesus

Another element in the Acts helps to bring out the continuity between the experience of Jesus and that of the Christian. This is the presence and the role of the *witnesses* to Jesus. This word, that holds such a large place in the book, is perhaps a creation of Luke. However, it develops an ancient evangelical tradition according to which Jesus, before going to His death, confides to His own the mission of giving testimony to Him in the tribunals (Mk 13:9), of adducing in public trial the important facts that will confound the accusations and manifest the innocence of Jesus, the accused. Such is likewise the meaning of the witness borne to Jesus by the disciples in Jn 15:26 and 16:8-11. In Lk 24:48 and in the Acts, the role of witness is broader and tends to be confused with that of apostle, charged with announcing the Good News. It is necessary that the witness have accompanied Jesus during His life in order to testify that Jesus risen is indeed the Jesus who was crucified (Acts 1:22). All aspects of the evidence are inseparable: the witness for Jesus is one who has followed Him "from the time of John's baptism" (1:22), who saw Him risen (2:32; 3:15; 5:32; 10:29.41; 13:31), who appears in court to testify in favor of the accused. It is the cause of Jesus that Peter and the Twelve have to defend before Jerusalem and the high priests when they pretend to reopen His trial (5:28).

In the use of the word *witness* an essential fact appears: the preaching of the apostles is not only the telling of the facts to which, given the circumstances, they alone had access.

It affirms the continuity between the old experience, the sharing of the earthly life of Jesus, and the new experience, that of the Risen One. At the same time, it shows that after the resurrection the word of Jesus, His power, and His liberty now pass through the hearts and mouths of His witnesses. Those who, while their Master was alive, had abandoned and denied Him, now, far from Him and alone, before the same tribunal, take on His attitudes and declarations. Their experience derives from His.

The Holy Spirit effects this experience.[1] The Acts bring out the fact that this Holy Spirit is given by the Father to Jesus so that through Him the Spirit may be poured upon all flesh (2:17.33). The Holy Spirit is not an impersonal gift, however valuable. If His person seems indistinct, incapable of being set apart, exteriorized, incapable of being contemplated in Himself, this is not because He is weak or hazy. Quite the contrary, He can give life to those in whom He dwells. If Jesus gives the Spirit, He imparts the very power which makes Him live.

C. The Disciple As a Continuation of Jesus

This is another characteristic of the Acts, doubtless peculiar to Luke rather than to his sources. It surely goes back to an ancient experience, attested to by Paul; and it is a part of his own experience. There is a sort of identification between Jesus and His disciples. The Jesus who appears to Paul on the road to Damascus is "He whom you are persecuting" (9:5); it is to the Lord that they adhere by joining the community of His disciples (5:14); and it is the Lord who through their words and the example of His followers adds new Christians to the community (2:47). This continuity is particularly noticeable in times of persecution. It does not depend simply on the permanency of an identical situation. Not only do we find the same adversaries, nations, and peoples united against Jesus and His disciples; we find the same vocation, the same Word to be delivered (4:27-29). Stephen, dying for having made confession of Jesus, resembles Jesus in His death (Acts 7:56-60; Lk 23:34-46).

The clearest example is Paul's last journey to Jerusalem.

Luke in a striking, even surprising, manner stresses the parallelism between Paul's journey from Tyre and that of Jesus going up to Jerusalem (Acts 21:15; see Lk 9:51). Like Jesus, Paul knows he is going forward to a painful destiny, that he is to be "delivered into the hands of the Gentiles" (Acts 21:11 and Lk 18:32; see Acts 28:17). Like Jesus, he sees rising up against him the multitude of his fellow countrymen shouting for his death (Acts 21:36; see also Lk 23:18).

D. Conclusions

The Acts, evidencing a long and complex evolution, yield two apparently dissimilar perspectives. In the discourses of the first part of the book, the experience of Jesus is seemingly absent, whereas the experience of the disciples, that is, conversion, is brought about by an intense gaze upon the person of Jesus, the pattern of His life, and the mystery of His relationship with God and men. Beginning with these ancient texts, Jesus is the one and only center, the convergent point of faith and life, whereas what He himself experienced is not brought to our attention. Surely the collective nature of these texts, where only what is essential is mentioned, must be taken into consideration; and generalizations must be avoided. Nevertheless, compared with these selections, the pages where Luke recounts Paul's actions, particularly his return to Palestine, the termination of his third journey, and his arrest, testify to an experience in which the person of Jesus, His sufferings, His prayer, have become deeply personal to Paul. The difference is incontestable.

However, we must note that these references to Jesus and His experience are attributable to the author of the Acts, who makes reference to his first book, the Gospel. That in itself indicates that this relationship to the experience of Jesus was for Luke, and doubtless for Paul, a vital experience. It does not disclose the experience of Jesus himself. This will be the function of the Gospels.

Chapter II

Saint Paul

Paul's situation is a good example. He did not know Jesus, and during His earthly life he did not believe in Him. Once Paul comes in contact with the risen Lord, his life is changed: "Indeed I count everything as loss because of the surpassing worth of knowing Christ Jesus my Lord. For His sake I have suffered the loss of all things, and count them as refuse, in order that I may gain Christ . . ." (Phil 3:8). This decisive experience induces a complete change of attitude. Jesus and His death and resurrection are at the heart of this experience (3:10). It cannot be doubted that Jesus is the beginning and the end of this new life. But is there any relation between Paul's experience of the risen Lord on the road to Damascus, and the experience of Jesus Himself during His life among men. E. Güttgemans sees no relationship with the earthly life of Jesus, but rather an immediate and fundamental relationship of Paul with the risen Lord.[1]

According to E. Käsemann, Paul's sufferings constitute, as it were, an *epiphany* of Christ.[2] The paradox of strength manifested in the weakness of His apostle indicates the identity between the earthly Jesus and the glorified Lord. This epiphany is in the here and now. It does not refer to Jesus in His earthly life, nor does it refer to a risen Jesus existing in glory as the world develops. The death of Jesus is the advent of eschatological time; the power that shines forth in the weakness of His disciples brings out the correspondence between the Crucified and the power of God. We recognize in this interpretation, both coherent and abrasive, the vigor of Bultmannian thought.

Nevertheless, this synthesis seems forced. That it exploits with rigorous logic basic affirmations of Paul is incontestable: "... as it is my eager expectation and hope that I shall not be at all ashamed, but that with full courage now as always Christ will be honored in my body, whether by life or death" (Phil 1:20). "I will all the more gladly boast of my weaknesses, that the power of Christ may rest upon me" (2 Cor 12:9). "From now on, therefore, we regard no one from a human point of view; even though we once regarded Christ from a human point of view, we regard Him thus no longer" (2 Cor 5:16). But this way of thinking omits several texts nonetheless significant, where the experience of Paul is supported by the experience of Jesus before His death. We may divide these texts into three groups.

A. Jesus Gives Himself Up to Death

There are texts in which Paul, in order to justify his behavior or the behavior he suggests to those to whom he writes, refers to the behavior of Jesus when He gave Himself up to death: "For the love of Christ controls us, because we are convinced that one has died for all; therefore all have died. And He died for all, that those who live might live no longer for themselves but for Him who for their sake died and was raised" (2 Cor 5:14-15).

"I have been crucified with Christ; it is no longer I who live, but Christ who lives in me; and the life I now live in the flesh I live by faith in the Son of God, who loved me and gave Himself for me" (Gal 2:20).

"... and hope does not disappoint us, because God's love has been poured into our hearts through the Holy Spirit who has been given to us. While we were yet helpless, at the right time Christ died for the ungodly. ... But God shows His love for us in that while we were yet sinners Christ died for us" (Rom 5:5-8).

"He who did not spare His own Son but gave Him up for us all ..." (Rom 8:32).

"And walk in love, as Christ loved us and gave Himself up for us, a fragrant offering and sacrifice to God" (Eph 5:2).

"Husbands, love your wives, as Christ loved the Church

and gave Himself up for her ..." (Eph 5:25).

All these examples refer to the Passion, not to a definite episode of the Passion, but to the interior decision that was the starting point of the Passion, whether this decision is presented as coming from the Father, as in the two passages from the Epistle to the Romans, or whether it is a decision made by Jesus. Moreover, in all these texts the recalling of the Passion points to a present situation. The intention is not to arouse imitation,[3] but to bring out the present action of Christ and God. In all the passages note particularly the very frequent and explicit mention of love. Love brought into play at this moment sets in motion an irreversible situation. It does not call for an equivalent response, yet for the believer it brings about a discovery and establishes a new life.

Three of these texts seem to be built on the same model "... loved ... gave Himself ..." (Gal 2:20; Eph 5:2.25). J. Gnilka,[4] commenting on the Epistle to the Ephesians, thinks it is probable that there is here a question of a well-known expression, an echo of which we find twice in the First Epistle of Peter in this typical form: "... for Christ also suffered for you, leaving you an example" (2:21); "For Christ also died for sins ..." (3:18). Doubtless the remark is worthy of interest. It would prove that the anonymous Christian faith to which these texts refer was contemplating spontaneously in the Passion of Jesus the expression of an attitude and an interior decision, and that the faith was based on that experience. It would prove also with what ease Paul was able to exploit this theme, and, as a consequence, to what depths he lived it. Obviously, for him this interior evocation of the Passion is not to be ascribed to a knowledge according to the flesh that he disdains or condemns: "From now on, therefore, we regard no one from a human point of view; even though we once regarded Christ from a human point of view, we regard Him thus no longer" (2 Cor 5:16).

B. The Way Chosen by Jesus

A second series of texts places Christian behavior in relationship with another experience more difficult to describe and situate historically, but which appertains to what is most profound in the person and life of Jesus: "For you know the grace of our Lord Jesus Christ, that though He was rich, yet for our sake He became poor, so that by His poverty you might become rich" (2 Cor 8:9).

". . . let each of us please his neighbor for his good, to edify him. For Christ did not please Himself; but as it is written, 'The reproaches of those who reproached you have fallen on me'" (Rom 15:2-3).

"Have this mind among yourselves, which you have in Christ Jesus, who, though He was in the form of God, did not count equality with God a thing to be grasped, but emptied Himself, taking the form of a servant, being born in the likeness of men. And being found in human form He humbled Himself and became obedient unto death, even death on a cross" (Phil 2:5-8).

The passage from the Epistle to the Romans can be related to the preceding series. However, we place it here because even if it evidently refers to the Passion, which is confirmed by the reference to Psalm 69, one of the psalms used in this context in the Gospels and the Acts, it characterizes less the fundamental decision of Jesus to give Himself up to death than a permanent attitude. The other two texts present a number of difficult questions. Nevertheless, it seems clear to us, as it does to the majority of exegetes, that the two texts are related and have the same perspectives. In the one from Philippians, Paul is repeating a hymn to Christ already known to the members of his communities. Both texts presume a pre-existent Christ and a decision on His part setting up for Himself His type of earthly life. This decision was translated into the type of behavior evident in the whole of His earthly life. There is a consistency between this constant behavior and the death willed and undergone by Him.

As different in aspect as these texts may appear in relation to those of the preceding series, more than one element connects them. They mention no event in the life of Jesus other than His death, but they are interested in the secret of this life and this death. They see this secret in a personal decision which then becomes an interior experience, a manner both singular and ordinary in the living of human life, a life of sacrifice, poverty, and obedience. They, too, see in this choice and experience of Jesus the basis for the choices and experiences that are to characterize the disciples. Jesus did not give, strictly speaking, examples capable of being reproduced; rather He provided a starting point and the possibility of a new life, bearing the mark of Himself as He was in His humanity. Finally, these texts also seem to be rooted in language and expressions anterior to Paul, and announce a common faith.

C. The Mystery of the Cross

Another type of text is reflected by those that fix attention on the Crucified: "For I decided to know nothing among you except Jesus Christ and Him crucified" (1 Cor 2:2).

"O foolish Galatians! Who has bewitched you, before whose eyes Jesus Christ was publicly portrayed as crucified?" (Gal 3:1).

"But far be it from me to glory except in the cross of our Lord Jesus Christ, by which the world has been crucified to me, and I to the world" (Gal 6:14).

Doubtless, we may place in this series the typically Pauline line in the Epistle to the Philippians: ". . . death on a cross" (2:8).

What is striking here is the power of attraction that fixes attention on the cross. This is the cross of our Lord Jesus Christ. Between it and Him there is an indissoluble bond, and this bond can only be interior. This cross belongs to Jesus because He made it His own. This necessarily implies that in Paul's consciousness, in his interior, there is a relationship with the Passion of Jesus. Moreover, this relationship is explicit. It is his pride and glory. Just as Jesus made the cross His own through a free choice, so Paul does not withdraw his attention from the cross and its mystery. The wellspring of his activity, the power of his words, the essential experience in which he initiates his disciples are centered there. Once again in this series is verified the convergence of Christian experience and the experience of Jesus.

D. Paul As Image of Jesus

In the light of these three series of texts it is easier to give all their meaning to those passages in which Paul affirms the immediate continuity between his life, particularly his sufferings, and the Passion of Christ: ". . . as it is my eager expectation and hope that I shall not be at all ashamed, but with full courage now as always Christ will be honored in my body, whether by life or by death" (Phil 1:20).

"For I think that God has exhibited us apostles as last of all, like men sentenced to death; because we have become a spectacle to the world, to angels and to men. We are fools for Christ's sake . . ." (1 Cor 4:9-10).

". . . I die every day!" (1 Cor 15:31).

". . . always carrying in the body the death of Jesus so that the life of Jesus may also be manifested in our bodies" (2 Cor 4:10-11).

". . . I bear on my body the marks of Jesus" (Gal 6:17).

". . . in my flesh I complete what is lacking in Christ's afflictions for the sake of His body, that is, the Church (Col 1:24).

A common feature in these texts is the place the body holds and what it accomplishes. It endures, supports, suffers, and submits. Another feature is the public aspect of what it undergoes. A third is the importance of what takes place in the body; if it suffers as it does and in conditions that are somewhat scandalous, it is for the benefit of others, the Christians for whom Paul feels responsible. In all these features Paul's experience corresponds to that of the Passion. However, in another, it is distinguished from it. The Passion, as Paul contemplates and presents it, has something instantaneous and beyond time. It is on the horizon of Christian life, visible from everywhere, but always isolated in its uniqueness. The Passion as Paul lived it has a permanent element; it is repeated "unceasingly," "every day," in all situations, "be it by my life or by my death." It is monotonous and banal. And we may ask if the true Passion of the Lord is not precisely that. What would be the first Passion were it not repeated and accomplished during all the days of the disciple's life? As we have seen, such is exactly the conclusion of E. Güttgemans. The very nature of apostolic experience connotes the coexistence of power in weakness, revealing the very nature of the cross, its character as a primordial and eschatological event in the time of God.

All this is true and conforms to Paul's experience as he describes and announces it. But the preceding texts must not be laid aside; the experience of Christ Himself must preserve its exemplary value; and the constant relationship of Paul's experience with that of Jesus must also be retained. What Paul discovers in the paradox of his apostolate is not only the paradox and the changing of weakness into strength; in this transformation itself he perceives the very presence of the crucified and risen Lord. This is well expressed by the experience he describes to the Corinthians when he tells them how he discovered this paradox and assimilated it. It was in a meeting and conversation with the Lord: "Three times I besought the Lord about this [a thorn in the flesh], that it should leave me; but He said to me, 'My grace is sufficient for you, for my power is made perfect in weakness,'" (2 Cor 12:8-9). It is Paul's Lord who is with him and who, "living in him" (Gal 2:20), prolongs His own life in him.

E. Conclusions

Between the discourses of the Acts and the Pauline or pre-Pauline formulas, rich in meaning and experience, there seems to be a considerable distance. This fact, however, must not deceptively lead us to think that the Christian faith of the early years was very schematic and that it was only with time that it took on the characteristic of a personal relationship with the Lord. The simplicity of the discourses in the Acts corresponds with a real state of Christian thought, but it is the result of an artificial reconstruction. The richness of feeling and experience adopted or used by Paul cannot be explained without the continuity of a tradition. The experience of Jesus as it is recalled in these texts simply cannot be a later invention. For this reason, Christian experience, as it was understood more clearly, eventually gained the power to penetrate more deeply, yet always accurately, the initial experience that gave it birth, that is, the experience of the Lord Jesus Himself.

Chapter III

The Synoptic Gospels

Here it is not a question of giving a picture of Jesus as the Gospels present Him. What we are interested in is knowing what these texts will offer us concerning the lived experience of Jesus. At first, this attempt may seem misleading, if not futile. Indeed, one factor stands out conspicuously: the Gospels furnish us with extremely short and fragmentary data on this experience; and this data requires critical verification.

A. Personal Reactions of Jesus

The Gospels, notably the Gospel according to Mark, relate a certain number of reactions that let us see in Jesus a deeply human spontaneity. Mark notes Jesus' look on the group that surrounds Him (*periblepsamenos*). According to the circumstances this look shows every shade of the familiar reflexes. There is the look of compassion for the leper (Mk 1:41), of anger for the Pharisees (3:5), of attention and attachment for the disciples (3:34), of curiosity to discover who touched Him (5:32), a look full of the inexpressible for His own, disconcerted by the exclusion of the rich (10:23), a silent look at the Temple filled with sellers (11:11). Certainly this repetition shows a design and a method. Nevertheless, it is difficult not to discover in these glances the trace of a lived experience of which the memory remains deep.

Mark also notes other isolated, often very informative, reactions. For example, there is Jesus' astonishment at the incredulity of the people of Nazareth (6:6), His weariness before curing the epileptic child (9:19), His indignation against those who forbid the children to approach Him (10:14). Above all, he reports, as worthy of being noted, the fear, the anguish, the sadness that seized Him in Gethsemane (14:33-34). Through these notations, some of which may spring from generalizations, although the more significant ones cannot have been invented, there appears the countenance of a man with a very attractive personality and a human destiny both exceptional and yet very close to ordinary experience. But we cannot deduce from this any characteristics that would appertain to the unique personality of the Son of God and which would show an experience absolutely unique.

B. Self-Disclosures of Jesus

Confidences are rare, and seem to arise from exceptional circumstances. Jesus is scarcely ever confidential. He lives in close proximity to His disciples, but He does not gather them together to pour out His heart to them. This reserve makes the rare secrets He shares with them all the more valuable. Moreover, rather than secrets, we find glimpses of His mission and His future.

1. Awaiting the Passion

The words of Jesus that have the greatest appearance of confidentiality, properly so called, are those in which an event or a question arises and Jesus allows the death He is to undergo to be glimpsed, as well as the manner in which He is moving toward it. The explicit announcements of His death, even those reserved for His disciples (Mk 8:31), are not included in this series. They constitute instruction, in the real sense of the word; and this instruction surely implies a form of consciousness in Jesus, although it does not yield anything in regard to His experience. On the other hand, there are words that escape Him under the very shock of an event and that are not intended for an audience, but to express a deep feeling long restrained. "Are you able to drink the cup that I drink, or be baptized with the baptism with which I am baptized?" (Mk 10:38). "I came to cast fire upon the earth; and would that it were already kindled. I have a baptism to be baptized with; and how I am constrained until it is accomplished!" (Lk 12:49-50). . . . "Behold, I cast out demons and perform cures today and tomorrow, and the third day I finish my course. Nevertheless I must go on my way today and tomorrow and the day following; for it cannot be that a prophet should perish away from Jerusalem" (13:32-33). . . . "I have earnestly desired to eat this passover with you before I suffer" (22:15).

Each one of these words raises a number of questions; it is certain that, in relating them, each of the evangelists assigns a value to them with a particular significance, with a meaning that they had in the communities where they were transmitted. It is a fact, however, that they have kept the initial form of a confidence that cannot be a later invention since this form is really very rare in the evangelical tradition. Another fact also is that a particular content corresponds to this form; baptism, fire, cup, prophet—these words come to Jesus either from what He experienced in contact with John the Baptist[1] or from the Old Testament as He meditates on it in the light of His mission.

These confidences are peerless. They give to the consciousness of Jesus moving toward His death a firmness without which it would be inexplicable to us. On the one hand, His mind is too clear to ignore the power of the opposition stirred up against Him and the resources at its disposal, too discerning not to follow its plans and to be aware immediately of its decisions. On the other hand, He pursues this enterprise of His life and His death with the consciousness of a mission He always describes in connection with the Old Testament, with Moses, the prophets, and John the Baptist. In contrast with theirs, His is a transcendent mission. He has the unique awareness of being the apogee and the fulfillment of theirs. These conclusions truly grow out of these confidences and allow us to place this experience at a level never attained by other men. But do they allow us to plumb the depth of this experience and to find there a filial consciousness? We cannot see how.

2. *The Son As Revealer of the Father* (Mt 11:25-27; Lk 10:21-22)

With this word we go farther. Here Jesus no longer places

Himself in relation to John or the prophets, but directly to God, in a relationship that belongs only to Him, a relationship of reciprocity. This relationship is not only solemnly affirmed; it is lived in thanksgiving, in an exultation of joy and gratitude (Lk 10:21). For our subject no word of Jesus is more precious than this. It affirms both the unique experience of the "Son" and His will to share it. "The Son," an expression that certainly dates back to Jesus, tells us that He is the only one who can describe Himself by this word and that He can so describe Himself solely by His relationship to the Father. At one stroke, by pairing the Father and the Son, Jesus proposes what He then explains: One only knows the Other and is known by the Other.

The value of this expression is further enhanced because it springs from a lived experience. Indeed, it seems that Luke (10:21) has preserved the original context better than Matthew (11:25), the link between the exultation of Jesus and the discussion with the disciples as they recount the success of their mission. The word that springs out in this fashion is explained more naturally, not as a declaration, but as a confidence at the moment when, in the presence of His own, Jesus allows Himself to be seen in His most profound mystery, living under the gaze of His Father and finding His joy in returning that gaze. It is the same élan that reveals Jesus in thanksgiving in the presence of His Father and that leads Him to share the secret of His joy with the very little ones.

This confidence has an almost immeasurable greatness. Not only is it the bursting forth of a feeling too strong to be contained, but it manifests also the need to communicate wholly, to have others share His own experience. "Whoever receives from God, and in conformity to the divine Will of the Son, the revelation of God's message, that one enters into the same relationship with God as Jesus who knows the Father."[2] The only limitation that can possibly be pointed out here is that this revelation is described from only one side, by the one who communicates it. Moreover, it must be noted well that Jesus Himself only speaks in this manner after the event, because He knew the effect of His presence in the world and He saw the Father reveal His mystery to the little ones. The lived experience of the latter is not described.

3. "Abba" (Mk 14:36)

J. Jeremias has shown the importance and significance of this word of Jesus.[3] It is a word from the vocabulary of childhood, a familiar name, about the equivalent of the expression "dear Father" that is not found in any known Jewish prayer; it must indicate a personal experience. D. Flusser nuances the significance of the above affirmation. "If Jeremias did not find the divine title *Abba* in the Talmud, it is because the elements of charismatic prayers are found rarely in rabbinical literature."[4] Flusser cites examples to show that the Jewish miracle workers, contemporaries of Jesus, declare that one is to call God *Abba*. These declarations are indeed precious and give evidence of a truly filial faith, capable of grasping the deep relationship between the child's confidence in its father and the confidence that God looks for in His children. If they dare apply *Abba* to God, they do so only after consideration and comparison, starting from *abba* as used by children. In the case of Jesus there is no justification, no explanation; the word bursts forth from His heart spontaneously. Doubtless, it is a recall from His childhood, at the period when, with Joseph and Mary, Jesus was becoming aware of His humanity as children do with their parents, and at the same time becoming aware of His very own secret, that His Father was Another.

The Gospels do not tell us how Jesus made this discovery, and He never said anything confidential about it. Nevertheless, the episode about Jesus in the Temple (Lk 2:41-50) is very valuable. It shows simultaneously with what naturalness Jesus lived as a child with His father and mother. "Your father and I," said Mary (2:48); and with the same naturalness He places over against them, "my Father" (2:49). In relation to the event itself Luke's report is late; however, it brings together facts that determine the only possible logic. If Jesus is truly the Son of God, He cannot become aware of it from anyone, not even from His parents, not even from the circumstances of His conception. If he were to learn from another what the Son of God is, then He is not the Son of God. If His personality is to be that of the Son of God, He must have that personality from His birth—or never have it.

No human being can imagine what the Son of God is. Mary herself can learn it only from Him and from seeing His life. No human words, no matter how subtle or precise, can show what the lived experience of the Son of God can be. If Jesus is the Son of God and if He is to say so some day, it is necessary that He have this experience from the beginning of His life, from the first awakening of His consciousness. It is not necessary that this consciousness when He comes into the world should be more advanced than that of other newborn children. All that is necessary is that Jesus, from the first moment of His life, through what He receives from the universe, from outside Himself, should live and feel grow in Him an infallible élan, the unmediated assurance of being enveloped by God with a unique love and of giving back a unique response. It is quite natural that this unique consciousness of the Son of God should develop in His experience of His parents and their love.

This childhood word, *Abba,* appears in the Gospels only during the agony in Gethsemane (Mt 26:39; Mk 14:36; Lk 22:42). It is not even a confidence, the sharing of a secret. It is a plea to His friends not to be left alone. It is the spontaneous cry of a child overwhelmed with anguish as it finds itself lost. Alone, yet within earshot, it is to His own that Jesus manifests all that He is.

Gethsemane is indispensable for the Christian experience of Jesus and reveals the fundamental paradox. Nowhere appears better to what a degree Jesus truly trusted Himself to men, to His friends, to their fidelity, and with what naturalness He lived in their presence the mystery that united Him to His Father. Nowhere else shines out better the radical powerlessness of man to receive this secret and to answer this communication.

C. Jesus Shares His Experience

If we had only these words of Jesus, if we were obliged to dig out their meaning and try to understand them, assuredly we ought to give up trying to enter into His experience. Then the Christian experience would be that of the disciples, careful to meditate on the teaching of their Master and to be faithful to Him. Now, according to the Gospels, the disciple had quite another experience, for he lived in the entourage of Jesus and was introduced to the experience of his Master. A reading of the Gospel necessarily goes beyond the words of the text and permits our entering into the concrete experience of Jesus as He lived among His own. "The function of the disciple is based on a life in common with the Master,"[5] and the Master's life is an experience into which He introduces His disciples. This stands out from even a superficial reading of the synoptic Gospels.

The Gospels do not propose a chronological plan, but they certainly do manifest the natural progression of a human life. Jesus goes through certain stages; His action includes different periods that flow naturally from one another and follow a curve that seems true to life. In the first period Jesus still seems close to John the Baptist, a replica, as it were, of the great prophet. After John's imprisonment, there is the Galilean period, the proclamation of the Good News, the announcement of the Kingdom, the time of the messages from the Sermon on the Mount, a time of growth, the time of the parables of the sower and the growing harvest, the period of miracles and enthusiastic crowds. The multiplication of the loaves marks both the high point of this enthusiasm and the reserve of Jesus. The confession at Caesarea underscores the disparity between the illusions of the crowds and authentic faith. Then comes the announcement of the Passion, the moving toward Jerusalem, the hardening of the opposition, decisive explanations, the nearness of the end, the eschatological horizons. Finally, there is the conspiracy, the Last Supper, the Passion. The order of these events is coherent and logical. But this order, while offering no solid basis for reconstructing an exact chronology, is, however, very suggestive in order to understand the lived experience of Jesus and His disciples.

1. Jesus and John the Baptist

What was the presence and the activity of the prophet for Jesus? It is impossible to know this with certainty. We have an intimation, upheld by much verisimilitude, that John had a

profound influence on Jesus. To receive the baptism of John
could not have been for Jesus just a formality or a gesture of
deference. The Gospels begin the account of the activity of
Jesus after this event, and it is highly probable that this experience may indeed have been a major and decisive one.
In any case, we have no words of Jesus in relation to this
event. It is certain that the evangelists wish to present Jesus
at the time when God sends Him to carry out His mission.
Accordingly, since from this first day they confer on Him the
stature of the Son of God that the resurrection will reveal, it
would be useless to endeavor to discover what the experience
meant to Him. It is not useless to point out Jesus' memory of
John. By His manner of speaking of John, we can conjecture
what their meeting may have been. "Why then did you go
out? To see a prophet? Yes, I tell you, and more than a
prophet" (Mt 11:9). We perceive, too, that by looking at
John, Jesus knows He is there for another mission: "For John
came neither eating nor drinking ... The Son of man came
eating and drinking" (Mt 11:18-19). Perhaps, too, as E.
Lohmeyer[8] and J. Jeremias suggest, Jesus' reply to the prominent men who ask Him to justify His intervention in the
Temple (Mt 21:23-27), "The baptism of John, whence was
it?" (Mt 21:25), is significant. Is this more than a clever way
out, and does it express His conviction that His mission is
tied in with the baptism received from John?[7] Here we cannot
go beyond hypotheses, but it is important not to forget that,
just as Jesus served His apprenticeship as man at Nazareth,
He served His apprenticeship as prophet with John the Baptist.

2. The Good News of the Kingdom of God

After John the Baptist's arrest Jesus leaves the Jordan
country and begins to go about in Galilee (Mk 1:14). He
is dissociated from baptism and becomes the "evangelist."
There is a change of manner. Across the Judean desert people came to Him at the Jordan. Now He starts to seek out
men where they are living, suffering, and sinning. He chooses
twelve disciples: "... [He] called to Him those whom He
desired, and they came to Him. And He appointed twelve
to be with Him, and to be sent out to preach ..." (Mk 3:13-

14). John was preparing the coming of God and His judgment; he did not know in what this coming consisted or what form this judgment might take. Jesus, the evangelist, the herald who separates Himself from the group at the time when He will make His entrance into the city, belongs to a Kingdom that is coming, and where it is enough that the door be opened for His entrance. "The Spirit of the Lord is upon me, because He has anointed me to preach Good News to the poor. . . . Today this scripture has been fulfilled in your hearing." (Lk 4:18-21). Today "the blind receive their sight . . . and the poor have the Good News preached to them" (Mt 11:5).

Behind the words and the quotations, the reality must be seen. Jesus cured, and to do this He seeks those who suffer. He does this, not as a wonder worker showing off his powers, but as a witness of God's compassion and power (Mk 1:41; 6:34)—living among men, pressed upon by the crowds, overwhelmed by the ever new sight of misery and sickness, by the spiritual destitution of the crowds without a guide.

Seeing these sick cured, the crowds captivated, He Himself lives what He is announcing. He sees the birth of faith and thanksgiving. Simultaneously, He is on the side of God who cures and on the side of the unfortunate who finds life again. "This was to fulfill what was spoken by the prophet Isaiah, 'He took our infirmities and bore our diseases' " (Mt 8:17).

And Jesus admits His own into this dual experience, into the two facets of this experience, that is the coming of the Kingdom of God. They, too, will be able to cure (Mk 3:15; 6:13); they, too, will know the burden of misery (Mt 15:23) and the exhaustion of days among the crowds (Mk 6:31).

3. The Sermon on the Mount

Matthew (5:2) and Luke (6:13-20), each in his own way, bring out the presence of His disciples at the Sermon on the Mount. Moreover, both point up the presence of the very great throng, from the countryside, around Jesus and the disciples. This setting has a meaning: what Jesus is saying here is being fulfilled for the disciples who follow Jesus, but is the

same for every man wherever he is. This is not a secret instruction, reserved for an elite group; it is an experience to
be lived, and the sign that it is possible to be lived is that
from that time to the present it is lived around Jesus.

It is centered in Jesus because it is first of all lived by Him.
If the beatitudes are true, if the poor are happy and those
who mourn consoled, it is because Jesus is there and with Him
God's riches and joy. Traditionally, the beatitudes are a
sapiential form, a call of the wise man to others to profit by
his experience. In the Gospel they take on a prophetic tone,
because for Jesus Himself the Kingdom is only on the thres-
hold, and He is still awaiting it. He awaits it with the absolute
certainty of one who sees it coming. It is around this waiting and this certainty that He gathers His disciples.

For Jesus the secret of this certainty is the Father, His
Father. The Father knows the needs of His children and is
concerned about them even before they are (Mt 6:8.32); the
Father sees all their actions and knows their worth (Mt
6:4.6.18). Visibly, in this certainty of Jesus there is something
that cannot come to Him either from experience or from the
desire of always accepting the will of God. For Him it is a
fundamental proof that comes to Him from the deepest part of
His being and that governs all His actions. Now, all His activity consists in having His hearers participate in this certainty. It is not to be done by sharing with them the strength
of His conviction, or by imposing the proofs from evidence,
but by having them participate in His filial attitude. Constantly in the discourse recurs the refrain of what the love of
Him whom they know so slightly, and whom Jesus knows so
well, is for the disciples: "Your Father" (5:16.45.48;
6:1.8.14.15.26.32; 7:11). The formula contrasts clearly with
the "My Father" where Jesus expresses the consciousness of
a unique relationship with God (10:32-33; 12:50; 15:13;
16:17.27; 18:10.14.19.35; 25:34.41; 26:29.39.42.53). The
two formulas hold; and if Jesus can tell men who their
Father is, it is definitely because He knows who His Father is.
It is in virtue of His personal experience that Jesus calls His
disciples to live in His manner. They must share in His experience to have experience of the Father.

This experience of Jesus is simultaneously the experience

of God and that of man. In the sermon Jesus repeats un-weariedly the name of the Father, but His horizon from one end to the other is humanity.

He uses the most ordinary human experiences as examples: the daily cares about food and clothing, living with others, the annoying ones and enemies, the position a man seeks to hold in society, the elementary fabric of living. It is not necessary to adapt and make oneself understood before a simple audience. It is a matter of reality in all this teaching.

This is also evident in another important theme of the Sermon, that of the opposition between the Law and the Word of Jesus. When He places the Law in opposition to His Word, He does not at first view the will of God in this Law, but the Law as it is practiced among His people. This practice in itself is not to be condemned, but it does not correspond completely to what God placed in His Law, the breadth and exigency of which Jesus has come to explain. To show the meaning of the Law is not to abolish it (Mt 5:17); it is to reveal the plenitude of its meaning and at the same time indicate it as a starting point for a real life. Accordingly, life, and this existence, has its value, but to discover the Father is to discover a new meaning in the Law and at the same time in existence.

It is the same in relation to the place Jesus gives to "what the pagans do" (Mt 5:47; 6:32). He does not condemn them; He considers their behavior as typical of the current reaction on the part of the ordinary person. By that He certainly does not mean that the pagans are not capable of acting otherwise. He is speaking here of the "Law" in its sociological meaning, of what is considered the norm to which everyone habitually submits. Starting from this base, from this behavior that connotes roughly a common aspiration of humanity, Jesus brings out the true manner of responding to this aspiration. For Him, to experience the Father entails first of all living human life to perfection.

The Sermon on the Mount is something quite different from a pattern for life, however beautiful it may be. It is an action. It is part of Jesus' action, an approach through which He comes to announce and set up the Kingdom. The sermon tells what fills His days: to welcome, to listen, to accompany, to solace, to pardon. He does not say this for self-explanation and self-justification. He says it for men so that they may come to join Him and live with Him His own experience, which is simply that of man, a child of the Father. This unique experience of Him who alone can say "my Father," He offers to all, so that all, with Him, will be able to say "our Father" (Mt 6:9).

4. Jesus and Sinners

Jesus' manner of acting with sinners is a splendid indication of the bond between His experience and ours. His way of going to sinners is a striking characteristic. Whereas sinners would come to John the Baptist to confess their sins (Mk 1:5), Jesus moves about to find them. He Himself goes to find those who are shunned, publicans and prostitutes (Mk 2:15; Mt 21:31); He chooses one of the Twelve from them; He is seen in their company; He permits a sinful woman to touch Him lingeringly (Lk 7:39). This behavior, which is considered scandalous, Jesus proclaims as the very purpose of His mission: "I came not to call the righteous, but sinners" (Mk 2:17).

This characteristic behavior expresses the very mission of Jesus and distinguishes Him from all others. The sinners who seek out John ask him what they must do (Lk 3:10.12.14), and, indeed, this is the spontaneous movement that arouses all religious enthusiasm in order to find a way of overcoming the evil that corrupts the heart of man and destroys all his works. But Jesus does not come to say first what must be done. First of all He comes to pardon, because it is God's forgiveness that man needs first, and He comes to bring proof of this forgiveness; He eats and drinks with sinners; His place is there.

The forgiveness of sins implies a twofold experience, that of God who forgives and man who receives forgiveness. They are scandalized when they see Jesus forgiving sins, and the scandal springs from a just principle: "Who can forgive sins but God alone?" (Mk 2:7). For Jesus to be able to say, "Your sins are forgiven," He has to be absolutely sure of it. It is not a question of an exhortation to confidence, but an authoritative action; and to be absolutely sure of the outcome, He must have direct access to God and know with absolute certainty that God has decided to forgive.

Now for Jesus this certitude is tied in with His mission. He is in the world to testify that God forgives, and forgives because He has sent Jesus. This certitude is likewise tied in with His knowledge of God; God waits to forgive: all His joy is in forgiving. Here is, undoubtedly, one of the most basic experiences of Jesus as described in the Gospels. In it are harmonized the experience of what God is, what He Himself is, and what He is to do in the world. This experience is not foreign to His personality; quite the contrary, it expresses it completely. It is a spontaneous movement that draws Jesus toward sinners; it is a movement wherein He discovers an elementary reflex of normal humanity, the need to save what has been lost (Lk 15:6.9.24). Also it is a reflex of God, and only Jesus can assure us of it. Thus Jesus, by the spontaneous movement of His heart, because He is most natural, finds Himself expressing the very movement of God. It is one of the most striking signs of the unique bond that attaches Him to God and of the experience that constitutes His being. Always completely Himself in all His actions, totally free in all His decisions, He is in this very liberty the expression and revelation of Another than He, His Father.

An experience on the part of God, forgiveness is also an experience on the part of the sinner. Genuine forgiveness is not merely the action by which the offended person decides to forget the offense suffered. It is a meeting and a reconciliation, reinstatement, and restoration. The Gospel shows this. Jesus seeks the sinners, but these also go toward Jesus (Lk 7:37; 19:3); and the forgiveness is effected in the meeting: the sinner's discovery of Jesus and Jesus' discovery of what a forgiven heart experiences. The pardoned sinner, likewise, has a twofold experience: that of Jesus who forgives and the forgiveness that transforms him. The experience of Jesus on the part of the forgiven sinner is really tied in with what Jesus lives, because, through the forgiveness of Jesus, the sinner receives the forgiveness of God.

5. Caesarea: Communion with Jesus in Faith

The confession of faith at Caesarea shows in full light this meeting between the lived experience of Jesus and that of the disciple. It reveals the secret of this meeting and of this communication, faith. Matthew's version (16:13-20) is in this regard very clear. Doubtless it represents a composition of the evangelist, and we are surely closer to the initial event in Mark 8:27-30. Matthew's version, even if it has a certain artificiality, because of its synthetic completeness, attains an unsurpassable truth.

At Caesarea, Jesus asks His disciples to tell Him what He is for them. The question is somewhat surprising. Unless he were disguising himself for fun, who would dream of asking the question, "Who am I?" If we can understand that Jesus, precisely because He is not a man like other men, could ask this strange question, we do not understand at all how He can expect an answer. Either an answer is possible at the end of an inquiry, and this proves that Jesus is identifiable starting from known reactions and that therefore He is definitely a person capable of being classified within our categories, a man just as others are; or He is one whom no word can define, no category can enclose, the One who by definition escapes all identifications. There is no possible answer that could be true; all the answers would be untrue.

However, Jesus asks the question, and the question is real. Jesus is not having a lesson recited that He would have taught previously, as though He would wish to be sure that it has not been forgotten. For Jesus has not yet said who He is. It may be objected that the texts do not tell all and that nothing can be concluded from their silence. But there is no question of an occasional silence. The Synoptics bring to light a fact that cannot be just chance. Not once in the Synoptics does Jesus Himself speak to announce who He is. In the Gospels more than once there are formal declarations about His identity, but these always come from someone other than Him: the Father at His baptism and transfiguration (Mk 1:11; 9:7); the unclean spirits (1:24; 3:11); Peter at Caesarea (8:29); the crowd at His entry into Jerusalem (11:9-10); the high priest before the Sanhedrin (14:61); the centurion on Calvary (15:39).

Against the backdrop only of Mark, an author who writes to present the "Gospel of Jesus Christ, the Son of

God" (1:1), this persistent fidelity to a clear position implies a fundamental conviction and an essential fact.

Beyond the literary data that can only with difficulty be viewed as accidental, there is data that belongs to the very essence of the Gospel fact and to faith. The believer cannot confess who Jesus is if he does not hold this revelation from the only one who possesses the key to it.

He cannot have this revelation from the simple word of Jesus or even from a combination of His words and actions. Indeed to reveal Himself, it is not enough for Jesus to speak or even to act. It is necessary that His words be understood, that they be meaningful, and that their meaning be the same for the one who speaks and the one who hears. Self-revelation cannot simply consist in having a formula repeated, no matter how exact and perfect it may be, in the way in which a master has a lesson recited. We could imagine Jesus choosing His words, explaining them in order to forestall misunderstandings, having them repeated to be sure He was understood. But, would He be truly revealed? Doubtless He would have put unfathomable questions for the mind and would have enlarged immeasurably man's horizons. Ultimately, He would have been left in conversation with Himself.

For Jesus to reveal Himself realistically, it was imperative that men seeing Him live should tell Him what He was for them. It was necessary also that He should be in their eyes, not only a worker of wonders, a venerated master, an inspiring leader, but the presence and the appeal of God Himself. This is what Jesus' question helps them to discover. The people say of Jesus that He is an extraordinary person, a sort of marvel, something unimaginable, a resurrected prophet. From a being of this type one can expect anything; no marvel is impossible for him. But one has no true relationship with him; one can only enjoy passively his power and his caprice. Jesus is radically different from this mythical image. One can define Him only by beginning with a sufficiently real and deep experience. This is why Jesus' question is expressed only after a long period of life in common. Without being able to date the episode at Caesarea, it is clear that it is not close to the beginning of Jesus' public life, but can be placed at a relatively short time before the Passion, when the relationships of Jesus

with the Galilean crowds are becoming difficult and the opposition of His known adversaries is becoming obstinate.

When Peter says to Jesus, "You are the Christ" (Mk 8:29),
which certainly expresses the meaning of the original reply,
even with the explanatory additions of Luke ("the Christ of
God," Lk 9:20) and of Matthew ("the Christ, the Son of the
living God," Mt 16:16), he expresses simultaneously what he
has seen of Jesus while living with Him and what Jesus is for
him. Apparently, these are two different things, but in Jesus'
case they coincide. To be the Christ, for Jesus, is not play-
ing a role for a time and then relinquishing it later. It is not
a privilege that He has from God. It is a role, signifying that
He has been sent to save Israel and all humanity. This role
expresses exactly what Jesus is, One sent from God, carrying
out completely God's work in immediate and perfect communication with God. In itself the word *Messiah* could say
something else and mean only a human person taking on the
role of savior for Israel. But in the mouth of Peter the word
takes on its strongest meaning, even if at that moment Peter
is still incapable of stating precisely its complete significance,
all of which is brought out in the additions of Matthew and
Luke.

In saying that for him Jesus is the Messiah, Peter bases his
statement on what Jesus has been for him from the time he
has lived with Him. He follows all His demands and gives
himself to the work He is undertaking. This Jesus, such as
Peter sees Him, such as He is now, capable of inspiring crowds
and cruelly disappointing cherished dreams, is for Peter the
perfect expression of his God, the representative in flesh and
blood of all that constitutes his faith and hope. Peter cannot
find a new word to say what Jesus is for him, but what he
says has a meaning. The Messiah, all that Israel expects from
its God, all that for centuries has made it live in faith and
hope: Peter has found Him and proclaimed Him. Certainly,
this is not the Messiah of which Peter would have dreamed,
and it is to be noted that Peter is almost the only one to
recognize Him. However, he touches exactly upon the true
personality of Jesus, this real relationship with the Father and
His mission in the world. In this way Christian faith rests on
the percepton of the relationship of Jesus with the Father.

This perception rests on an experience and describes an experience. By confessing that Jesus is the Messiah, Peter gives meaning to what Jesus has had him experience since He accepted him as a follower. This does not define only his personal experience. If he, Peter, can speak in the name of the Twelve, it is because the total experience that Jesus has had him live since the beginning has validity for all people and for each man. In order that this confession may have meaning, it is necessary to give it its place, as coming after all the activity of Jesus, all His teaching, His manner of giving, by His gestures and His words, meaning to the life of man. Peter says what Jesus is for him, but all that Jesus did for Peter He did in view of all men; and for this reason Peter's confession has a universal value and can be repeated by all believers.

Peter's experience, therefore, rests on Jesus, and it presupposes the experience of Jesus. This appears still more clearly because of the way Jesus ratifies Peter's declaration, according to Matthew's text. Jesus makes known to Peter that his faith is given by the Father, but this in no way implies that Peter has experienced any exceptional illumination. For if that were the case, Jesus would not need to tell Peter the source of his knowledge. Now, if Jesus is capable of calling forth Peter's faith in this way by asking at the right moment the necessary question, He is also able to know exactly what Peter means and can corroborate his statement. It is here that in a definite way revelation intervenes, and it is the joint work of the Son and the Father. It is necessary that the Father act in Peter and enlighten him so that he may be able to receive the word of Jesus and give himself to Him. It is necessary that the Son, a man capable of speaking and making Himself understood, be there to tell Peter that he has seen correctly and that he speaks the truth. In this way the dilemma in which we seemed to be held is resolved. Indeed, properly speaking, Jesus is He whom no word can define or encompass since He is from God and has the dimensions of God. Nevertheless, He can be named justly, when, through faith, man recognizes in Him the living presence of God, His reality and His mystery.

6. *The Path to the Passion*

As soon as He has obtained from His own this act of faith,
Jesus tells them the destiny awaiting Him and which inevitably
will be theirs from the time that, by proclaiming Him as the
Messiah, they have pledged themselves to follow Him. He
cannot spare them the experience into which He has entered,
the expectation of His death.

The announcement of His Passion and the announcement of
the cross for His followers are inseparable (Mk 8:31-38).
This is because the disciple cannot be separated from the lot
of his master (Mt 10:24). Furthermore, the destiny of Jesus,
although absolutely unique, reveals nonetheless a basic human
experience.

If Jesus is destined for death, it is because the logic of His
thought and action places Him in open opposition to the official representatives of His people. What is at stake is not
a certain detail, some shocking reaction; it is rather the very
principle of the Sermon on the Mount, a certain detachment
from the accepted mentality and from the milieu that tends
to hedge Him in. What is at stake is the very form of Israel
and its role in the world. The Jewish authorities in Jerusalem
refuse what seems to them the ruin of their people; the Roman
authorities, preferring the political game to justice, will up-
hold this party. Long before dying, Jesus is condemned; and
He knows it.

What He finds facing Him, what He will see spread out
before Him the day of His trial, is the convergence and coali-
tion of all in man that goes counter to the truth. It is a new
experience of man that scarcely appears in the Sermon on the
Mount. This does not mean that Jesus ever naively supposed
man to be without sin. The Sermon itself speaks of hostilities,
adulteries, violence, and deals with real human beings. The
call of Jesus assumes that victory over evil is possible, and
He counts on what is best in the human heart. Jesus will never
deny any part of this call, and the Sermon on the Mount is
verified in all His actions up to His last sigh. The call that He
voices is not always understood, and at times Jesus encounters
stubborn refusals. He is to face up to failure, to refusal, to
a mad and pitiless opposition. He could escape this, and He

knows this up to the end (Mt 26:53), but He would fail the mission that constitutes His reason for living.

If we set aside the more or less explicit confidences concerning His death, as studied above, the announcements of the Passion in the Synoptics are found in two series of texts. On the one hand, there are a certain number of parables more or less explicit: the disappearance of the bridegroom (Mk 2:20), the murder of the beloved son by tenants of the vineyard (12:6), the tragic lot of the prophets (9:12-13), the stone which the builders rejected (12:10), among others. On the other hand, there are quite explicit announcements concerning the destiny of the Son of Man. J. Jeremias thinks that all of them stem from a single primitive Aramaic form that we can reconstruct with strong probability: "The Son of Man is to be delivered into the hands of men." Indeed, this form is the nucleus of all the announcements, the point of departure of diverse variants that remain very close to the initial model.

Now this model is instructive. It tells us the power and capacity for destruction of the men who will lay hands on Jesus and have Him killed, and the relationship established by God between this power of evil and the personality of the Son of Man. Such is indeed the meaning of the Passion, which the Risen One will reveal, but again by going back to a previous announcement. And such is also the meaning of evil in the world. Evil, and particularly sin, exercises in the world and will exercise on Jesus a fearful power. Jesus will find Himself defenseless before it and will succumb. The explanation of this scandalous fact is not definitively the power of evil; it belongs to the personality of the Son of Man.

Because He is the Son of Man, Jesus is to be delivered up. To understand this explanation, one must know the significance for Jesus of the expression *Son of Man*. A certain number of exegetes do not accept the idea that Jesus ever called Himself the Son of Man and maintain that this title was given to Him by the Judeo-Palestinian communities. It seems, however, much more likely that the term comes from Jesus. The strongest argument adduced by the critics who reject it is the distance that the texts establish between Jesus and the personage of the Son of Man expected on the clouds of heaven. For example, according to Bultmann, if it is true that Jesus an-

nounced the coming of the Son of Man, He did not identify
Himself with him.[8]

This argument can be answered easily. It is true that Jesus
places a distance between Himself and the Son of Man and
that He speaks of him in the third person, as someone other
than Himself. But this manner of speaking of him as of
another is so lacking in naturalness that it is difficult to imagine
the Christian community, if it is this group that invented the
identification of Jesus as the Son of Man, inventing likewise
the distance. This distance is much better explained if we recall what the personage, Son of Man, evokes in the Jewish
apocalyptic tradition. In this tradition it is a question of a sym-
bolic personage belonging to a world of celestial visions, whose
appearance and exaltation mark the coming to earth of the
kingdom of the saints (Dn 7:13-27). Naturally, Jesus does
not present Himself directly as the Son of Man as long as the
Kingdom of God remains on the point of coming. However,
all of Jesus' actions take on their meaning because they are
preparing this triumphant coming.

The fact that Jesus understands His existence in the light of
the Son of Man is a proof of His authentic humanity. He
knows where His mission is leading Him; He sees His enemies
about Him plotting His death; but He lives, like every man,
in expectation of the future that is approaching.

Jesus is an authentic man; and the inalienable nobility of
man is his power, even his duty, to freely project his life's
decisions into an unknown future. For the believer, the future
into which he projects and throws himself is God in His
liberty and immensity. To deprive Jesus of this opportunity
and to have Him go forward toward an end already known
and distant only in time would be to strip Him of His dignity
as man.[9]

Jesus cannot describe in advance the future that awaits
Him, but He knows that this future is to be found in the Scriptures; and He knows how to find there that which points to
Him directly. The personage, Son of Man, is, among all the
possible figures, the one He prefers. It does not imply any
particular earthly event, but solely the coming of the Kingdom. It entails a moving forward, a period that elapses before
the appearing of the personage whom Daniel's vision describes:

"I saw the night visions, and behold, with the clouds of heaven there came one like the son of man, and he came to the Ancient of Days and was presented before Him. And to him was given dominion and glory and kingdom, that all peoples, nations, and languages should serve him . . ." (7:13-14). This preferred choice shows that between Him and God there are simultaneously a distance to be bridged and an equality of greatness. Thus, in the celestial image of the Son of Man, Jesus contemplates the law of life that He is in the act of living on earth.

Jesus has His own way of interpreting the celestial vision of Daniel. All takes place as though He were systematically making the earthly details of humiliation and suffering correspond to the glorious characteristics of the vision. In the heavenly vision the Son of Man appears as judge; on earth, He is blasphemed, rejected, and delivered up. Between the two there is a close bond: if Jesus is not delivered up, rejected, and put to death, He is not the Son of Man; and He fails in His mission.

Jesus' statements about the Son of Man are not procedures of preaching and exposition; they present an original experience of the One who knows to what He is going forward, who knows that in advancing toward death He is fulfilling God's promises and that from His hands He will receive the victory. He knows He is exposed to all the cruelty of sin, but at the same time He will be faithful to God to the end and accomplish His work. In the predictions of the Passion, the expression *it is necessary* does not imply the fatality of evil. It means that in order that Jesus may be the Son of Man and appear in the glory of His Father, He will have had to know to its very depths the power of sin, the distress of a lost humanity. The victory of God is in this abyss.

7. The Last Supper

The Last Supper is the last prediction of the Passion. The evangelists introduce it by the basic theme: "The Son of Man will be delivered up . . ." (Mk 14:18-21). But here we see a complete reversal. He who is to be delivered up, whose death is already decided, whose life hangs upon the signal

Judas is to give to the chief priests, forestalls the hand that is going to seize Him and deliver Him to death. Jesus knows He is marked for death, and He freely forestalls that hour when He will be unable to act for Himself, and surrenders Himself. Not only does He do this to affirm that He knows and governs all, but particularly to show that those who deliver Him up cannot in their rejection go as far as He Himself goes in self-giving. At the table where Jesus is giving Himself, the accounts bring out the presence of "him who will deliver Him up" (14:20), and this simultaneity is essential. Handed over by a friend who eats at His table, Jesus bestows on His own His body, "given" (Lk 22:19; see 1 Cor 11:24), His blood "poured out" (Mk 14:24; Lk 22:20). An important difference is to be noted here. All His life Jesus has given His body to His own; today He is giving it to them unto the shedding of blood.

He thus accomplishes the word about the Son of Man proclaimed when He was announcing His Passion. Because He is the Son of Man, because His destiny as such is to know the sin of man to its horrific depths, He allows its work of death to proceed; at the instant when this work is going to triumph, He forestalls it and transforms it into a work of life, into a gift and nourishment. Certainly, such is one of the meanings that the Gospel account gives to the Last Supper of Jesus and the institution of the Eucharist. Nowhere in the continuation of the account will the evangelists go farther in showing what the experience of the Passion was for Jesus. It is at this hour, in complete liberty, in control of all His powers, that Jesus gives Himself to death. Here we see a more than prophetic action, for He is the one who here gives His word and who will keep it to the end. From this moment Jesus can no longer escape death. And this, not because of Judas and sin, but because of Himself and His fidelity.

This gift of His life that Jesus gives to His own is bestowed on them by sharing the bread and the wine. By this action Jesus institutes the New Covenant (Mk 14:24; Lk 22:20). In other words, He has these followers share a new experience. A covenant is a definite type of relationship with God. God's covenant with Israel had introduced His people to a privileged experience. The New Covenant does not abolish the former one; it is the unique Covenant lived to the end by Jesus, one that will be lived by those upon whom He bestowed the gift of His body and blood. The experience of Jesus, Founder of the New Covenant, and the experience of the disciples called to live the Covenant, necessarily converge. Sharing the repast signifies and effects this.

8. The Passion

What was the experience of the Passion for Jesus? On this point the evangelists show a very definite discretion. This does not imply that they have nothing to say or that they had no remembrance of it. But from the time of the suppliant prayer in Gethsemane up to His last sigh they have left us no confidential information, not one word by which Jesus would have shown what He was suffering and experiencing. Doubtless, there were few testimonies about these hours Jesus passed abandoned by all. Most certainly, the dominant Christian sentiment before the Passion which abounds in the first announcement of the Good News in the Acts and the writings of Paul is that of awe before a divine mystery, before a theophany more impressive than that of Sinai. Writing of the Passion, the evangelists stress above all whatever deals with revelation: in Mark, the revelation of the Son of God; in Matthew, that of the Parousia of the Son of Man; in Luke, the revelation of the Savior of the world. For all the evangelists, John included, the Passion shows forth the power and greatness of God, which, paradoxically, triumphs over all human powers. The evangelists do not forget the price paid for this victory, nor do they fail to bring out all that this event contained of iniquity, inhuman cruelty, and blindness. If we feel all through their accounts their gratitude and adoration, we also feel that they have nothing to add to the facts: these speak for themselves.

The words of Jesus that would let us have a small idea of what He is experiencing at this time are those given us by Mark (15:34) and Matthew (27:46): "My God, my God, why have you forsaken me?" A cry of frightful distress, this is a cry that we could call desperate were it not addressed to "my God," thus maintaining the indissoluble bond. Moreover, it is almost impossible simply to imagine what is hidden in this cry. In any case, it is to minimize it without reason, if one considers that it indicates only that Jesus on the cross recited Psalm 22, the psalm that begins by this call for help, but ends on a note of triumphant confidence. What is certain is that the Gospel quotes only the beginning. If the writer is so bold as to attribute to Jesus such a declaration that would seem to justify all His enemies by declaring that God is no longer with Him, it must be that he feels himself bound by an unquestionable tradition. In the perspective of the accounts of the Passion, it seems nevertheless that the main intention is to bring out the total failure of Jesus.

All His pretensions, one after the other, are contradicted. He called Himself a prophet greater than Moses, and yet He cannot say who strikes Him (Mt 26:68). He claims to be the Christ, the king of Israel: "let Him now come down from the cross" (27:42). He declares He is the Son of God: "let God deliver Him" (27:43). Doubtless the evangelists in this way allow us to capture something essential in the experience of Jesus crucified: the complete ruin of all He tried to do in His lifetime. To gather together disciples, to awaken in His people a new meaning of God, to set up an era of justice and peace—of all that had been the objective of His words and actions, nothing remains. Essentially, the perspective that made Him tremble when He announced His Passion was that of being delivered into the hands of men. That is what it is to be the Son of God.

At this hour, nevertheless, the Son of God reveals Himself to the world, and the centurion on guard proclaims: "Truly this man was the Son of God" (27:54). To die in this way, to cling to God in this total abandonment, to be up to the moment of death what He had been during His whole life, at the service of all humanity, offered to every man, free from all resentment, for this He would have to have been the Son of God.

Before the Son of God on the cross, in the presence of this failure and abandonment, it seems that the only possible attitude is silence. What human experience could possibly match His? This solitude in which Jesus dies, with the few women who have remained faithful to Him "looking on from afar (Mk 15:40), cannot be penetrated. How could there be anything communicable between man's experience and His?

However, this death in the sight of all has a meaning. It speaks to all who see it. It is a theophany corresponding to that of His baptism. Matthew's Gospel seems to have wished to multiply the parallelisms,[10] but Mark already brings out what is important. The veil of the Temple is rent just as the heavens were opened at the Jordan (Mk 15:38; 1:10); and the words of the Father, "You are my beloved Son; with you I am well pleased," are paralleled in the confession of the centurion: "This man was the Son of God" (1:11; 15:39). Therefore this death, the death of this man, the manner of His death produce faith. As at Caesarea there was communication between what Jesus lived and what Peter said, here there is communication between His Passion and the faith that accepts it. The object of this faith, at the cross as at Caesarea, is the confession of the unique and unbreakable relationship that unites Jesus to God.

9. The Resurrection

The Gospels do not allow us to enter into the experience of the risen Jesus. This is a world where man does not penetrate, the world of the invisible God, that in which Jesus dwells and into which He disappears after each apparition (Lk 24:31.50). The apparitions last no longer than is necessary for faith to recognize Jesus. Their purpose is to show that He is the same, that the resurrection has not changed Him, that He is, indeed, He who used to eat with His disciples and that He remains intimate and unpretentious with them. This is an absolutely necessary experience, for no one would ever have imagined the Risen One with these characteristics. The Risen One recalled by Jesus' announcements would be either the Son of Man coming on the clouds of heaven (Mk 8:38) or the shepherd rounding up the sheep (14:28), both figures of divine dimension.

The words of the risen Jesus are not at all confidential or even like conversations; they do not disclose His reactions. When He speaks to the disciples of His Passion on the way to Emmaus, He does not go back to His dramatic experiences.

He repeats the teachings He was accustomed to give. As soon as His disciples have their faith renewed, He leaves them, entrusting to them their mission: "Go" (Mt 28:19). Thus, the experience of Christian faith in the Risen One is not the discovery of a new person; on the contrary, it is the discovery of the identity of the Crucified and the Risen One. And if He who was crucified has risen, this fact is of interest to all mankind and is to be announced to every creature.

Chapter IV

The Gospel of John

The majority of the indications that will be found in this chapter are already presented and supported by proofs developed in the article on St. John the Evangelist.[1] This is due to the special character of the Fourth Gospel. It is the Gospel where the author has given most of himself and of his personal experience, and where the lived experience of Jesus, His personal behavior, His spiritual lineaments hold the major place. In this Gospel is found solved in the most positive and almost overwhelming manner the question central to this article: "Is there any communication between the Christian experience and that of Jesus? Without answering explicitly a question John would not have suspected, this Gospel attests that for its author the answer would be positive. The opening of the First Epistle of John, very similar to the prologue of the Gospel, proposes a continuity between the communion of the Father with the Son, that of the Son with His witnesses, and that of these last with their brothers in the faith (1 Jn 1:3). All the development of the Gospel moves toward the prayer in which Jesus asks the Father that the love enveloping Him may live in the hearts of His disciples (Jn 17:26).

This view, that seems obvious to the author and inspires all his work, raises a few questions. It hardly seems to coincide with the views of the Synoptics. The latter, as we have just seen, assuredly take for granted the communication between Jesus' experience and that of His disciples, but they find it in faith, in a faith that scarcely dreams of dwelling on what it experiences and on the experience of Jesus, but simply

tries to listen to His word and to accomplish His will. If
John's Gospel shows a similar distance in relation to the experience of the Synoptics, may we not wonder if John has
not added much of his own to the experience of Jesus, such
as He was in the midst of His disciples?

A. Jesus' Experience

A striking feature of this Gospel is the place allotted to
the personal experience of Jesus. He speaks in the first person much oftener than in the Synoptics (upon opening a con-
cordance, one realizes this), and to this must be added all
the times He designates Himself as "the Son" (3:17.35.36
[twice]; 5:19 [twice], 20.21.22.23 [twice]; 6:40; 8:35.36;
14:13). Even if it is very probable that 5:19-20a may be
taken for "a father . . . a son"[2] and that Jesus is using a most
human experience to clarify His relationship with the Father,
it is manifest that He is thinking first of all about the latter
and refers to it continually.

Jesus' initiative is another indication of His personal
presence in this Gospel. The Jesus of the Synoptics does not
lack this feature: He leaves the Jordan to go to Galilee (Mk
1:14); He chooses some disciples (1:17); He leaves Caper-
naum to go elsewhere (1:38), and so forth. Many of the
episodes in the Synoptics simply find Jesus in a certain place:
and it is men, the sick, the crowd, His enemies, who set the
action in motion. But from one end to the other of John's
Gospel, it is Jesus who initiates and controls the action. As in
the Synoptics, He meets others; people come to find Him so
that He will intervene in some situation (Jn 2:3; 4:47; 11:3).
But although Jesus goes straightway with the centurion (Mt
8:7) or Jairus (Mk 5:22), according to John, whether with
His mother, with the royal official, or with Martha and Mary,
He waits before making His decision. In John it is rare that
Jesus should be somewhere without His having made the
decision Himself. This control appears strikingly in evidence
at the time of His arrest (Jn 18:1-12). Even when the
evangelist does not stress that Jesus knows exactly all that is
happening to Him (1:48; 2:25; 4:18; 11:4.42; 13:1), his
whole account shows Jesus proceeding with complete con-

sciousness of His actions and their meaning. Others may be governed by events, their time is not too important, whereas Jesus acts only when His hour has come (7:6).

On more than one occasion Jesus explains the meaning of His behavior. Often His explanation only clouds the issue, but He so acts deliberately in order to lead His questioner into the mystery. One of the constant schemas of this Gospel is the dialogue in which Jesus begins with a surprising or miraculous action (4:7-9; 11:6) and then explains this action in terms of His mission and person: "My Father is working still, and I am working" (5:17); "I am the bread of life" (6:35); "As long as I am in the world, I am the light of the world" (9:5); "This illness is not unto death; it is for the glory of God, so that the Son of God may be glorified by means of it" (11:4). The majority of these solemn declarations "It is I . . ." are prepared by a progression in which an initial action and word combine and clarify each other in order to end by a final statement.

All these features manifest in Jesus a clear and permanent consciousness of what He is and what He is doing. All are linked with the affirmation constantly repeated in diverse forms that Jesus lives with His Father, as D. Mollat writes, "a vital relationship of His whole being . . . a mysterious symbiosis translated in terms of union, of total and constant presence of one to the other (5:20; 8:16; 16:32), of one in the other (10:38; 14:10), of mutual knowledge (10:15), of reciprocal clear glances (5:19-20), of absolute communion both of thought and of will for unreserved exchange (16:15; 17:10)."[3] All this commentary is exact throughout and can lead to only one conclusion: Jesus lives His relationship with God in a complete fullness and light that He alone can know. However, He speaks of it and makes it known.

The Synoptics point out twice Jesus' way of naming Himself "the Son" and of placing Himself beside His Father, but this is always in a passing way, either because He is moved by emotion and astonishment (Mt 11:25-27), or because He is urged by the logic of an argument (Mk 13:32). And if John and the Synoptics are in accord on this point, nevertheless a serious question remains. How does it happen that John has multiplied these situations so rare in the Synoptics?

Above all, how does it happen that he gives to these moments such importance that he builds on them his account and his work to such a degree that for him Jesus' action always consists in having His questioner face this affirmation, which, in one form or another, is the same? Is it not to systematize arbitrarily a procedure which in the Synoptics appears otherwise flexible and much less planned? For an answer to this question, it is necessary to study the experience of the disciple as found in John's Gospel.

B. The Disciple's Experience

A quick glance would seem to indicate that the answer Jesus waits for from His hearer is just one word, *faith*. John's Gospel has been written so that those for whom it is intended may believe (Jn 20:31). It starts at Cana, when for the first time His disciples believe in Jesus (2:11), and is completed by Jesus' word to Thomas: "Have you believed because you have seen me? Blessed are those who have not seen and yet believe" (20:29). This whole drama takes place in the presence of Jesus. It may be said that it is a simple experience.

Upon further consideration we see that this faith is extremely rich and complex. D. Mollat points out that for John believing is recognizing and welcoming, seeing, hearing, and even touching, tasting, and perceiving; and it is also meeting and knowing Jesus, choosing and following Him, and, ultimately, it is loving Him.[4] A general view of this Gospel shows it is a succession of meetings of Jesus with diverse persons from all directions and from varying environments. There are the wedding guests at Cana, Nicodemus in a nocturnal conversation, the crowds at the multiplication of the loaves, the Temple theologians, the important persons of Jerusalem. The alternatives are always the same: either receive the words of Jesus with faith, or reject them. But the approach is different each time, depending on the persons, the situation that has come about, and the witnesses present at the discussion.

In general there are contrasts among varied groups, in which are juxtaposed all shades of meaning, all conditions, all types of reactions, and the permanence of a basic question. There are very diverse scenes where it is impossible not to be aware of the echo of definite recalls of places that still remain in the memory, and the repetition of the same adventure each time. There is a spiritual finesse that gives each chapter a special accent, that brings out the depth of all the words and illumines the hidden areas where lives are led. Nevertheless, all seems simple because the axis is always the same, always a question of the same thing, the meeting of Jesus with men.

The whole of this Gospel is made up of meetings between persons. John names many more persons than the other evangelists, to such a degree that some have spoken of "the individualism of the Fourth Gospel."[5] There are meetings with groups or great crowds, with the important people of Jerusalem, or with "the Jews," as John calls them, in his way of personalizing an anonymous crowd. On one side there are human beings, friends and enemies, Jews, Greeks (12:20), Romans (11:48), the world of that time; on the other side there is Jesus. In all its dimensions this Gospel has infinite perspectives, but never for a moment does it lose sight of the unique event that it is to describe, that is, the meeting between Jesus and men.

An art so conscious of its techniques may awaken suspicion. It is evident that this art consists partially in the use of style and structure. But the whole question is to discover in what this style and structure consist. Comparison with the Synoptics brings out considerable differences. Perhaps it also permits the perception of a deep relationship and a genuine continuity.

C. The Revelation of Jesus According to John

Jesus in John's Gospel usually speaks a language different from that ascribed to Him in the Synoptics. He describes at length His relationship with His Father, frequently announces His heavenly origin, makes known to all the gifts He brings, life, light, truth. He stands before men and calls them. However, He is not really different from the Jesus of the Synoptics. We are not forced to accept this simply on the grounds of an intuition that might deceive us, so accustomed are we to a certain image of Jesus, combining, whether we wish it or not, the Johannine and Synoptic characteristics.

For John and the Synoptics the manner of self-revelation is basically the same. As was noted above, in the Synoptics, Jesus never declares His identity; and His revelation is authentic because it consists in Jesus' leading one along the path of faith. At the end of this path the disciple confesses with faith the identity of Christ. In John, it seems just the opposite. The statements in the first person, the "I am" expressions, emphasize like refrains the whole development of the account. Yet, in his way, John goes along with the Synoptics. The "I am" affirmations of Jesus appear normally at the end of a discussion or a dialogue called forth by an action of Jesus.

Again, each time Jesus rises in His greatness and shows forth His light, but He does not do this immediately. Nearly always He waits for the question to be asked, in order to give a clue to the discussion. At one time it is the Samaritan woman who herself asks the question (4:25). At another it is His enemies who oblige Him to explain why He cures on the Sabbath; it is because "My Father is working still" (5:17). At other times it is a miracle and the danger of its being misunderstood and exploited that obliges Him to clarify the issue: "Do not labor for the food which perishes, but for the food which endures to eternal life, which the Son of Man will give to you . . ." (6:27). Another time His enemies themselves bring about a decisive response: "We are descendants of Abraham . . ." ". . . before Abraham was, I am" (8:33.58). There are Martha and Mary, who expect all from their friendship with Jesus, but who do not yet know who He is: "Lord, if you had been here, my brother would not have died . . ." "I am the Resurrection and the Life . . ." (11:21.25).

This approach, not in the least a stereotyped one, is very different from a clever pedagogical procedure intended to arouse the curiosity of the pupil, or a calculated trick waiting for the moment to make an impressive declaration. It expresses the action of genuine faith and is expressed in a manner different from the Synoptics. In order that Peter should confess, "You are the Christ," the interior action of the Spirit, the gift of the Father, was necessary. It was also necessary that Jesus through His manner of speaking and living with Peter and the Twelve, through the bonds He was establishing with them—in other words, through His ongoing dialogue with His disciples—should have led them on the way. Peter's confession is unthinkable without the consciousness of Jesus who prepares and brings it forth, who enters upon the way and forestalls misinterpretations, lays bare illusions and calls upon faith. From the time He chose His disciples to live with Him, Jesus had been revealing Himself to them. The Synoptics do not say this, although they imply that for Jesus this required great patience. Those who were then making their way did not realize this hidden toil. If later on, when they announced the Good News, they became aware of it, they had no intention of recounting their own story.

It is this story that John's Gospel recounts. He tells it from the viewpoints of Jesus who reveals Himself and of the man before Him. John unveils the interior action that reveals Christ to faith. At the beginning, it is always Jesus taking the initiative. He knows who He is; otherwise no one would ever find out. Progressively, step by step, through all events, the alternating acceptances and rejections, He teaches those who follow Him to observe Him, to see Him live, to note the place God holds in His life, to discover that for Him God is all, and that they are in the presence of the Son and His Father. This is the way Jesus reveals Himself. Basically, it is the same in John as in the Synoptics.

Nevertheless, there are significant differences. The Synoptics, in a way, only describe a single revelation, that which all the disciples experienced from the time of their first meeting up to the resurrection. This is, if we may so speak, an experience common to all, both anonymous and official. It is the experience of the Twelve and of their spokesman, who can speak for the whole community. John, on the contrary, selects a certain number of different experiences, of various types and conflicting outcomes. Undoubtedly in this selection there is a mixture of elements impossible to isolate. Deep memories, situations, absolutely assured facts on one side— and on the other, a series of designed stylistics. Above all, there is the figure of Jesus Himself, who from the very first has the definite characteristics of the one totally self-revealed and fully accepted by faith. Hidden in the anachronism there is a profound truth: not only was Jesus from that moment the

Jesus whose cross and resurrection, the Passion and Pentecost were to reveal. But from that moment He was working
and revealing Himself in truth. Without the Johannine figure
of the Revealer, the revelation of the Jesus of the Synoptics
is not truly explained.

In front of Jesus, there is man: there is the response from
man. Even if the evangelist makes up an expressive and
varied gallery of humanity, his real interest is elsewhere, that
is, in the meeting itself. This meeting shows less what happens
in the individual than what he gets from Christ when he accepts Him, and what he misses by rejecting Him. Under the
different words—*see, hear, listen, feel, taste*—all showing
shades of faith, John thinks less of describing an experience
than of portraying the unique fullness, the unimaginable wonder of the person of Jesus. Thus, Jesus, who has all His power
at the beginning of the revelation, who leads on as the Way
and illumines as the Light, is likewise the Word who makes
known His glory, the Truth that satiates, the Son who shines
with the Father's love, the Bridegroom who fascinates those
who see Him. "The Revealer is also the revealed."[5] The experience of faith is wholly concentrated on the countenance
it discovers, and from this comes all its richness.

Apparently we are far from the Synoptics. They do not
ignore the transforming power of faith: the centurion of Caper-
naum, the sinful woman in Simon's house, Peter at Caesarea—
all do exactly what John describes. However, the Synoptics do
not think deeply about this. John contemplates and studies
the face of the Lord. This explains the particular accent of
his Gospel, which uses a language that belongs only to him.
The difference raises a question. Is this John's language, or
does John attribute it to the Lord?

D. The Experience of John and of Jesus

The Jesus who speaks in John is so different from the one
who speaks in the Synoptics that we are tempted to see in the
whole of this Gospel a personal construction, a magnificent
meditation arising from interior fidelity and spiritual intel-
ligence. Such is Jesus, as faith sees Him and as He is portrayed by a believer whose whole world is built around Him.

This is an extraordinary testimony of the power of Jesus on a heart, but wherein is this testimony a Gospel?

Here we must not make a mistake. John, who so constantly has Jesus speak in the manner of a revealer, gives us no more confidences about Him than the Synoptics and makes no pretension of admitting us to the depths of Jesus' soul that would have remained hidden from the other evangelists.

All Jesus' words about Himself and His work are not confidences, but public and solemn statements. They do not disclose the state of soul of the living Jesus, but rather the divine secret He is in the act of revealing. The evangelist never deceives his reader. He always has Jesus speak before an audience, at least before the Twelve. Even the conversations after the Last Supper, with all their familiar tenderness, remain discourses, declarations destined for a public and made to be transmitted. In this Gospel, therefore, one must not look for a personal experience, however lofty or brilliant it may be. In Christ, as John presents Him, one must not look for a person unknown to the Synoptics. The Johannine portrait of Jesus is not due to any extraordinary and privileged revelations. It springs directly from the common experience of faith.

It is not possible to trace the evolution of John's language and style or to distinguish what is to be attributed to Jesus or to the evangelist. We can only indicate the procedure followed, starting from faith. To believe is to discover who Jesus is by discovering what He does; it is to feel oneself led and nourished by Him: Paul would say "seized." To the degree that one advances, he discovers that more and more he only follows and responds; accordingly, more and more one looks at Him, listens to Him, observes Him act and speak. All that Jesus says in this Gospel, John heard by living his faith in his Lord.

This faith is a communion. The words that express and accompany it all speak of contact, meeting, closeness. He who believes dwells in Jesus and Jesus in Him. Perhaps because he is more active, Paul feels dispossessed of himself and filled by the one who dwells in him (Gal 2:20), so that for him the Christian experience becomes the very experience of the Lord living, working, and suffering in him. John does not take his eyes off the one who is before him, and union is achieved in this exchange: "Abide in me, and I in you" (Jn 15:4).

This communion in the lived exchange with Jesus is revelatory, and John discovers the import of Jesus' language: "my Father," "the Son." He does not have to imagine the communion between the Father and the Son on the basis of his communion with Jesus. On the contrary, he knows that all in this communion comes to him from Jesus; and by accepting this gift he hears Jesus say to His Father: "... You, Father, are in me, and I in you ..." (17:21). John, as he comes to understand the communion he lives in his experience, which derives from that of Jesus, discovers with amazement the depth of Jesus' own experience and the glory of God's only Son.

Chapter V

Modern Interpretations

From the collective data of the New Testament, it is difficult not to conclude that there is a link between the experience of the believer and that of Jesus. Christ is contemplated as the Crucified by Paul, as the Prophet of the Kingdom of God by the Synoptics, and as the Word in His mission as Revealer by John.

These differences are one of the reasons for the diverse views regarding the relationship between Jesus and His followers, even among those who profess Christian faith in Jesus. Aware that this presentation contains a large amount of schematic simplification, we can, nevertheless, distinguish a certain number of typical positions.

A. Immediate Contact

In spite of considerable differences and sometimes irreconcilable oppositions, we find in the great representatives of liberal Protestantism and the principal Catholic exegetes faced with Modernism, a somewhat similar way of looking at Jesus, of trying to reach, beyond the words and actions, the profound secret of this unique person. It is a look that wishes to be simple and immediate. It does not ignore the methods of the critics and the problems raised, nor does it disdain scientific demands and methods. The actual result of criticism is to bring out the personality of Jesus, which personality is the heart of faith, whether in the liberal interpretation, where it represents the highest and the inexhaustible source of humanity's religious experience, or in traditional faith, where it ex-

presses the very person of the God made man. The positions
may be in opposition, but the orientation is the same. One
may compare Léonce de Grandmaison († 1927) and Adolph
von Harnack († 1930), in their attempt to capture the most
expressive and original characteristics of Jesus:

> This unique combination of assured confidence with
> the most profound sense of religion, of an inborn and
> tender familiarity that needs no forgiveness on any
> score with a supremely clear realization of the horror of
> sin and the demands of justice, of undisturbed security
> with an infallible sense of what God is and what we
> are, constitutes one of the doors by which we may gain
> admittance to the mystery of Jesus . . .
>
> If we attempt to sum up the Saviour's inner life by
> its most striking characteristic, we shall perhaps decide
> on what I may be allowed to term its limpidity. It has
> a sincerity which can be reconciled neither with selfish
> exaggeration nor with vain promises . . These indications
> allow us to sum up our impressions in the word that
> the great Genoese mystic, St. Catherine Fiesca Adorna,
> used by choice to express all that she beheld in God—
> *nettezza.* The inner life of Jesus offers the most beautiful
> picture of the pure fullness of the divine Being that it
> has ever been men's privilege to behold.[1]

> The dominant note [in Jesus] is one of silent recollec-
> tion. He is always Himself, always tending to the same
> end. He never speaks in a state of ecstasy, and in Him
> the tone of prophetic exaltation is rare. Charged with
> the highest mission, His eyes and ears are always alert
> for all impressions of life about Him. What a proof of
> deep peace and absolute certitude! . . . He who has no
> place to lay His head does not speak as a man who has
> severed all ties, as an ascetic hero, as an ecstatic prophet,
> but as a man who possesses interior peace and calm and
> who is able to give them to others. His speech is power-
> ful; He places before man a formidable option, leaving
> him no means of escape. However, what is most
> frightening is that He seems to take it for granted and

he speaks of it as something natural in the language of
a mother speaking to her child.[2]

From different viewpoints these two texts express the same
conviction of the ability to find in the Gospels the living Jesus
in the uniqueness of His experience, and this is definitely the
foundation of faith. In simpler language M.-J. Lagrange
(† 1938), in finishing his great synthesis of the Gospels, traces
the same itinerary:

> The Gospel contains teaching, but not a teaching by
> philosophic formulas, abstracted from time and place . . .
> The Gospel is a reproduction of a fact, the actions and
> words of Jesus, a fact naturally complex and vital, con-
> taining the usages, the way of thinking and feeling of the
> Jews in the time of Tiberius. Jesus did not write a
> treatise on God, He did not even give any lesson in this
> subject. He spoke of the impending reign of God, al-
> ready begun. He made it understood He was the Messiah
> but did not define the meaning of the term . . . As it
> stands, this testimony in general is very clear; by way of
> the divine sonship of Jesus it leads us to His equality
> with the Father. At the very least, therefore, it will be
> necessary to admit that the evangelists were so per-
> suaded, as well as Saint Paul and the apostles who agreed
> with him, and the Christians converted and taught by
> them. This is what they called the Gospel of Jesus
> Christ.[3]

Today such texts seem out of date. What seems inadequate
is not the principle they affirm, for that seems to be in accord
with the analyses we have just made: there is a communication between Jesus and His disciples. What raises a doubt
would be the level at which this communication is established.
Is it certain that this attention fixed on Jesus, this admiration
before the richness and balance of His personality, do not
risk building around Him, like a magic cloak, a wonderful
setting that would prevent our reaching Him in His reality?
It is not a question of suspecting the faith of de Grandmaison
or Lagrange; it would be an elementary lack of realism and

gratitude to disregard the value of their work and the services they have rendered. To wish to examine further the question of the stage at which this communication between Jesus and the believer is established would be, doubtless, to show fidelity to their spirit.

The testimony of the Gospels on this point seems to us more definite and unquestionable than the proposed interpretations. That the human personality of Jesus played a major part in the attachment of His disciples to Him is indisputable. But for the authors of the Gospels this motive is never stressed. Faith is the only motive they emphasize. We take for granted too hastily that Jesus revealed Himself to the disciples through confidences and direct teaching and that it was sufficient for them to listen and repeat well. Now, the Synoptic tradition gives as essential data that Jesus never, even at His trial, declared explicitly that He was the Christ or the Son of God and that the messianic confession at Caesarea is a happy discovery received from God. This revelation is established beyond any doubt because it does not come from mental categories and verbal teaching, but from an experience of lived faith, expressed in front of Jesus, then explained and confirmed by Him. This process leaves all their worth to the valuable observations of Harnack and de Grandmaison, and we may even think it justifies them, for it is through this familiar contact with Jesus that the disciples progressively perceived what was unique about Him and how He could be the Messiah promised by God. However, at the heart of this experience there remains the confession proper to faith, that in Jesus, God gives really and totally what He has to say and to give to humanity.

B. Unbridgeable Gap

For Rudolph Bultmann faith is the only possible contact with God. Faith, as Bultmann defines it, is incompatible with the fixed attention on Jesus as we find it in Harnack or Lagrange. For these, observing Him live, listening to Him speak —this is the natural means of penetrating His mystery and arriving at faith. For Bultmann this contemplation is only an illusion and an obstacle to faith. It comes from the "fleshly"

desire of knowing Jesus according to His natural individuality
(2 Cor 5:16), which is a rejection of knowledge in the Spirit
and which corresponds, in the intellectual order, to the rejection in the moral order of the pretense of being justified by
works.

What can the experience of Jesus have been? Is there such
a thing as a "faith of Jesus"? To these questions there is no
acceptable answer. They arise from the ever present tempta-
tion that substitutes for faith our response to the peremptory
questioning of God, the need to know and to objectify, all
of which changes the word of God into a mythological discourse. Doubtless, the New Testament contains a certain number of texts that clarify precisely these points, but literary
criticism shows their secondary character; and authentic in-
telligence about the Gospel message permits their being
"demythologized." "Is the decision demanded by Jesus' message the echo of the decision that concerned Jesus Himself?
. . . Perhaps it is exact, but what good is this type of thinking that can come only from a biographical interest?"[4]

R. Marlé, in his *Bultmann et l' interprétation du Nouveau
Testament,* exposes R. Bultmann's thought in this way:
"Christ is, we do not know why, the human organ of God's
word. That is all. His very person is without mystery and
without any particular relationship with God who sends Him."[5]
Bultmann replies clearly: "Indeed, it is all, and I think it is
quite enough. The expression 'we do not know why' very
clearly betrays the wish that theological reflection on the
'mystery' might later ground the reasons of faith. It betrays
an effort to disclose the incognito of Jesus (speaking as Kierke-
gaard does) and, as a result, to destroy the paradox of the
Word made flesh."[6]

For Bultmann, this willed indifference to the real personality
of Jesus is essential to faith. Studying what Christ is for Paul,
Bultmann thinks that for him Christ is not a master who
brought the world a new concept of God, or a model who has
given his conduct as an example, or a hero who has incited
human efforts to their farthest limits. If He is now the master
and model, it is not because of what His life was, but because
He is now the Lord. "Every concept of the life and death
of Jesus as a heroic human work is reduced to nothingness

by the fact that it is the Crucified who is preached. Every exaltation of the personality of Jesus fails and must fail because it would be only a 'knowledge according to the flesh' in both meanings of the expression: seeing Christ as a phenomenon observable in the world . . . and understanding Him according to the flesh."[7]

Must we say that between the earthly Jesus and the Lord acknowledged by faith there is no connection, no continuity? Bultmann does not say this, but his detailed remarks are more subtle to interpret than his negations. To the degree we can attempt to synthesize Bultmann's thought, often expressed in fragmentary style, we can say that for him this continuity between Jesus and the believer is observed in two ways, from the side of Jesus and then from the side of faith brought about by the death and exaltation of the Lord.

1. Jesus

If it is useless to pretend we know the secret of Jesus' consciousness, it is, nevertheless, possible to reach the consciousness Jesus had of His message and mission. Jesus knows Himself as from neither the past nor the future . . . His action is in the space between. His judgment on the present has its source in the personal consciousness of His mission. Therefore, He finds it in Himself. This judgment is not, as it will be later in His community, based on a reference to any event that could have been decisive for Him.[8]

Jesus taught no doctrine about His person, but without doubt He placed some emphasis on His person as having a certain importance, something definite, in so far as He wished to be the bearer of God's decisive word at the last hour.[9]

2. The Community

Not only is there an historical continuity between the death of Jesus and the preaching of the primitive Church, but this continuity is very deep. Not only does the community take up the words of Jesus; it has the same "self understanding" as Jesus and announces the same message: "Jesus of Nazareth is the eschatological event that submits all men to the judgment and grace of God."[10] To make Jesus the subject of preaching implies that there is given to His person a definite role and significance. "Such an appeal in regard to His person implies a Christology which assuredly is neither speculation on a celestial being nor the building up of a pretended messianic consciousness."[11]

It is easier to know what Bultmann rejects than what he affirms, and one still wonders how, after his rejection, he can still maintain his affirmation otherwise than in the pure paradox of faith. One can at least agree with him (and this is indeed for him what is important) that, on the one hand, Jesus is conscious of announcing the supreme word of God at the last hour, and, on the other hand, that the community took up His message and His words. Just the same, it is a fundamental continuity, and it would be markedly grounded and justified if Bultmann were to accept what appears as an immediate corollary of what he affirms. In order that Jesus may know that His word is the word of God, supreme and decisive, must it not be that He has access to God's supreme and definitive decision? Now, this decision depends on no event in the world, and it has no real meaning for any prophets of this world. Jesus can receive it from God alone, and it can have no meaning apart from His coming. To confess that Jesus is the only Son of God is assuredly to say more, but first of all it is to say that He has received His knowledge from God.

C. Identity within Difference

Karl Barth († 1968) is in certain respects the exact opposite of Bultmann. For him the Scriptures in their totality and immediate meaning are the word of God; the Gospels let us witness the very experience of Jesus Christ, the Son of God made man. The great adversary of Barth is liberal Protestantism, and Barth would repudiate as profanation all communication between the consciousness of Jesus and that of the believer that would be brought about by natural influences and psychology. For him, and he agrees with Bultmann here, the only Christian experience is faith. In this experience, man receives positively the gift of Jesus Christ, His life, His holiness, and His person. Thus in dialectic theology, we see, as co-existing, man the sinner deprived of the experience of God, and the justified Christian in whom Jesus Christ lives today and forever His personal experience.

"What God did yesterday in Jesus Christ, could it no longer be His action today and tomorrow, or be no longer a present or future action, except in the form of a distant effect on what was produced one day? . . . How can the present and future state of Jesus Christ be different from the state of existing, acting, speaking, suffering, and triumphing in the history that was formerly His? . . . His past coincides with all possible presents and futures."[12]

To understand what Jesus' life means, necessarily framed as it is in time and prolonged through all time, so as not to consider it a myth, one must be careful when Barth speaks of the life of Jesus, because he is thinking about the substance of that existence, of what he calls His being or His action:

> It is in His history, that is, in His life, thought of as His *action,* that Jesus existed for the community of the New Testament, that He was for them both present and future. His whole being in its effect on them and the whole world was identical with His entire action.[13]

This life of Jesus, that is an action and an experience of man and of God, is positively given to us. It is given to us by someone other than ourselves, for we do not possess it; but it is really given to us in our human condition, for it was lived by Jesus in our condition.

> Jesus Christ, the Stranger who lives another life, eternal life, is one of ours; far from being opposed to us He is in our midst. He shows that God's life is our life, that the life of grace is grace bestowed on all men, that eternal life is the real life promised and destined for us. His life is a human life like ours, lived in the midst of other human lives; as such it is our poor life, lived for us, invested and crowned with the promise of another life. The true objective, the positive meaning of the

encounter with Jesus Christ, is not to have us discover
that we do not have that other life, but to show us that
it is given to us in Him.[14]

These categorical affirmations leave no place for doubt.
Between Jesus' existence and ours the relationship leads to
identity. His life is really given to and shared with us. The
affirmation is so absolute that it raises a question. How is this
possible? What is hidden under these words? For Barth the
question is normal, and the answer is evident. It is the very
affirmation of faith; and this affirmation does not require
verification: it calls for belief. This faith is not simply the af-
firming of what is humanly impossible; indeed, it contains an
experience, and Barth's emphasis shows in what this experience consists. It is liberation, pardon received, life lost and
saved, the very experience of which the Gospels give testimony. Is it necessary to search further?

D. Revelation within Mystery

In his *Meditations on the Person and Life of Jesus Christ,*
Romano Guardini († 1968), by intuition, by contrasts, by
certain ways of approaching his subject, endeavored to present
a substantial consistency to the communication between Jesus'
experience and that of the Christian. Guardini is as convinced
as Bultmann of the uselessness of attempts to present a
portrait or a psychology of Jesus. But his conviction is based
on a radical affirmation, the divinity of Jesus.

Any attempt to show a psychology of Jesus is simply
impossible. One might, if required, present a psychological portrait of a Francis of Assisi . . . This would be
an attractive undertaking, made possible by laying bare
the roots of this remarkable personality, by describing
certain aspects of His life, the apparent contradiction
and deep harmony of the spiritual energy of this soul . . .
It is impossible to do this for Jesus except within extremely unpretentious limits. Even to attempt it would
be to destroy the authentic image of the Master, for at
the center of His person there is the mystery of His

divine sonship that precludes all 'psychology'... Only
one thing may be attempted: to show, from different
points of view, that all the qualities, all the characteristics of Christ lead to an impenetrability that is an infinite plenitude.[15]

In all the passages in which Guardini's approach is evident,
his gaze upon the lived experience of Jesus seeks to catch
what is unique and inaccessible in Him. We may point out
a few sentences in which the author tries to describe Jesus' behavior during His last days as He goes to His Passion.

He puts all His energy into the accomplishment of
His mission. He goes to meet men with arms and heart
open. He does not think of Himself. He knows neither
enjoyment, comfort, fear, nor compromise. He is absolutely and exclusively a Messenger, a Prophet, and
more than a Prophet. Notwithstanding, we do not have
the impression that here is a man who envisages a definite
goal and seeks valiantly to achieve it by His work...
We only penetrate further into the soul of the Lord if
we observe His actions and behavior from a central
point of view, situated beyond the world. As soon as
we place His existence in a category familiar to us, all
true knowledge vanishes.[16]

There is no fear in the soul of Jesus. This is not only
because He is naturally courageous, but also because the
center of His being is beyond what could be feared. On
this account one cannot speak of Him as being daring
in the human sense of the word. He is simply free, completely free, for what is to be accomplished at each
moment. He accomplishes it with sovereign and incom-
prehensible calm. We could continue these distinctions
at some length. The result would be only the confirma-
tion of what is already apparent. Here human measure-
ments are insufficient to appreciate what is happening.
It is true that here all is thought by a human mind,
willed by a human will, experienced by an ardent heart,
magnanimous and tender, but sprung from a source and
accomplished with a power placed beyond what we can
call human.[17]

The two statements are essential and must be kept together: there is a human form of Jesus, a human experience
accessible and given in the language of man, communicated to
men; but the center of this experience is at once real, incontestable, present and inaccessible, humanly impenetrable.
Now, for Guardini, it is precisely this impenetrable center that
allows Jesus to be in communication with all that is human,
to know this in His heart. "No one is for man what He is.
He knows the Father as no one else knows Him ... It is also
in this way that He knows men, in the very source of their
humanity. More perfect than any other man, He is closer to
man than anyone else."[18] There is something more. It is from
this fathomless experience that the very form of Christian experience is born, what it has simultaneously of the humanly
common and the inexplicable. This theme recurs several times
in Guardini. "Jesus Himself is the interior form of all that
is Christian."[19]

> The form that makes a Christian Christian, that which
> is to be manifest in all his actions ... is Christ living in
> him. This form acts differently in each one according to
> his nature. It does not show itself in a man as in a
> woman ... Its action differs according to times and
> situations, joy or suffering, work or encounters. But it is
> always He ... Christ lives His life anew in each Chris-
> tian. First it is the child and it develops until he reaches
> the age of a grown Christian; but his growth is that of the
> faith and love of a Christian, that of the consciousness
> he has of his Christian condition; it is the ever greater
> depth and seriousness with which the Christian con-
> forms himself to his ideal.[20]

Apparently, these lines show nothing very original, and for
each word one can adduce a sentence from Paul. In Guardini,
however, they have a special resonance. Guardini's meditation explores and verifies what Paul states without dreaming
of explaining. It marks the continuity between Christ and the
Christian on the most central and most mysterious point. If
the experience of Jesus can become the form of Christian experience, it is not because of an exceptional God-given privi-

lege; it is in virtue of His very nature. Beginning at Pentecost, the Church's experience testifies that Jesus, ". . . exalted at the right hand of God, and having received from the Father the promise of the Holy Spirit, has poured out this which you see and hear" (Acts 2:33). All the actions of the first disciples indeed show the typical reactions of Jesus. The explanation is there and immediate. Who is capable of creating in man a personality that leaves intact his consciousness and his liberty, and at the same time have it to be the personality of God, if not the Spirit of God? It is this basic certitude that Guardini's attention and thought explore. Enriched with the whole heritage of Christian meditation, sharing the new questions of his time, he constantly goes beyond the psychological observations, where piety risks being enclosed, in order to bring to light the mystery of Jesus. This mystery is not an evasion or an avowal of ignorance. It is not a simple affirmation impossible to control. It is formulated and verified in the very experience of faith. "The presence of Christ in man is Christian interiority."[21] The mystery of Jesus that R. Bultmann wishes so much to safeguard is here more than preserved.[22] It is the sign of the divine presence, the mark of the Spirit, the possibility of a real communication, an authentic experience of Christ in faith.

E. Jesus' Experience As Theophany

Today the most advanced thought on the relationship between Jesus' experience and that of the believer is without doubt that of Hans Urs von Balthasar. It constitutes one of the great themes of his master work.[23] This thought is truly theological and constitutes an interpretation of revelation with the aid of certain essential categories. The interpretation never loses sight of the scriptural data and the experiences they contain.

Jesus' lived experience, or, more exactly, the experience that constitutes Jesus, is in the nature of a theophany; what is more, it is a unique theophany. "In the Old Testament, men experience theophanies in the course of which they see, hear, and contact God in their way. But Jesus is the theophany *par excellence,* which this time goes as far as the Incarnation.

That is why God seen, heard, and touched in the man Jesus is at the same time the man who sees, hears, and touches God."[24] Saying that Jesus' experience is the theophany *par excellence* and that it is simultaneously an experience of God lived by man and an experience of man by God, is not simply placing Jesus at the pinnacle of an exceptional series. For the few major theophanies of the Old Testament are not without relationship with the common experience of Israel. All Israel's faith is, in some way, contingent upon the Mosaic theophany, and every believer who lives by this faith participates in turn in this theophany. He also sees, hears, and touches something of the God of Moses. Jesus' experience is both unique and unifying. Balthasar states that it is an archetypal experience.[25]

The theophanic experience of Jesus pertains to His humanity; it is not a memory or a transposition of a "divine" experience, for this would plunge us into mythology. "The affirmations about Jesus' experience of God must not, therefore, be interpreted as if, in His 'revelation' of God (Jn 1:18), Jesus was making statements about what He saw and heard in God 'before' His Incarnation. They really express what He, the Unique One who comes from God, learned by experience about God by His coming from and return to God. That is why these experiences are inseparably divine and human, not first divine to be later transposed into human language. This would be the Platonic doctrine of pre-existence and reminiscence."[26]

This experience of God in Christ is not situated above or outside His experience as man, as a sentiment, a super-rational intuition. By the function it assumes it is lived in the movement that sustains all His action. It is translated into all He hears, all He sees, all He does. In a few cogent lines Balthasar tries to let us see this unique experience. He has recourse to traditional dogmatic language, but by situating these words in their place, in the place where they first appear, in the gaze of faith directed upon Jesus by the authors of the New Testament.

> Christ as man is at the same time authentic man and man taken up into God. As authentic man, He is not a superman; rather, He is the perfection of a creature,

with the distance from God proper to a creature . . . He is also the perfection of the ancient relationship of the Covenant of the elect (the people and the individual) before the face of the God of the Covenant. In this sense Christ possesses the archetypal *faith* and the obscurity it implies in our relationship with God. This relationship is enveloped in a still thicker veil, in virtue of His expiatory taking on of the *sinful condition* of man . . .

But as man taken up into God, Christ necessarily participates in the consciousness of Himself as eternal Son, eternally coming forth from the Father and returning to Him. This participation is reflected in the human consciousness of Christ to the degree He experiences *interius intimo suo* [in the deepest part of His being] this consciousness of the Son, and, opening Himself to it, He possesses it. But again, because He is authentic man only by being man taken up, He also understands His authentically human experience of God as an expression and function of His divine Person, of which He is nevertheless humanly conscious only in the functional movement of His mission, in such a manner, therefore, that His humility and effacement are at the same time the expression of the divine will of kenosis. Consequently, the man God's experience of His creaturehood is, as such, an expression and function of His trinitarian experience. Or, again, the experience of distance in relation to God, which in Him is archetypal faith, is, as such, the expression of an intratrinitarian experience of God from the viewpoint of the distance that separates the Persons.[27]

This important text permits us to understand, first of all, how Christ can humanly live the experience of God, and also why He can communicate this experience. This arises from the fact that His experience is that of a man who lived in our condition and in our categories. Again it arises because it is the experience of the God who comes to unite Himself to man and to save him. Because it is the experience of the God who comes to man, Christ's experience is that of the Mediator; therefore, in essence it is communication. This is seen by the very place Jesus holds at the end of the line of prophets and at the beginning of all missions in the Church. "Being the Word Incarnate (and ceaselessly incarnated), He Himself attests what He says, by His whole life, so that His experience of God can be corporeally reproduced, because of their contact with His corporeal life, by the men who deal with Him and believe in Him."[28]

On the part of Christ, this communication of the experience He has of God implies that it is pure dispossession; on the part of man, this possibility of receiving Jesus as an expression of God is grace: "Jesus, the man, therefore, understands Himself (and learns self-understanding more and more) as what He is: the Word of the Father addressed to the world, whose real mission is that of the grain of wheat, to die for the world and in this way to bear fruit. Herein, He experiences God, not in an 'objective' vision, apart from His own reality, but in a humility that does not reflect on itself ... and leaves, within, all to God, and experiences in His own functional reality the reality of God who sends Him, disposes of Him, and begets Him eternally. This is why humility, poverty and simplicity will always be for Him the condition allowing Him to have others share His own experience of God."[29]

This text holds the answer to Bultmann's difficulty, which, in the name of faith, rejected the possibility of an objective experience of Jesus that does not deteriorate into mythology. All changes if the experience lived by Jesus Himself, His 'consciousness of self,' is the call that sends Him on His mission, and if He Himself is the answer to that call.

From this experience of God by Christ comes the Christian experience in faith, which is grace, that is to say, the communication of what is incommunicable: "This passage of what is incommunicable to communication is necessarily the result of the whole structure of the relationship of Christ with God. That this structure exists is due to grace that implies, according to its very concept, the sharing of that which is absolutely unique. The passage lies in the fact that the man, Christ, is the one who sees God as He is seen by His Father, i.e., as one who is sent, and that, for this reason, the one who sees Him, sees the Father ... This faculty of seeing what Jesus is in reality is ... the sight given by grace to man so that all that is human in Christ is the word, image, manifestation, and expression of the Father."[30]

The view of the person of Jesus which Balthasar proposes to us is one that, without sacrificing anything of the immediate notion that impels the Christian to welcome the Gospel vision with a simple heart, accepts completely the legitimate critical demands of modern man. This Jesus is not the mythical projection rejected by Bultmann, but, being entirely and in all His life a response to the call of the Father, He is at the same time a communication to men of this call. This Jesus appears capable, as Karl Barth affirmed without being able to explain it, of being down the centuries what He was during thirty years among us and of bestowing on believers the gift of His life and action. This Jesus, whose consciousness of self is at the same time pure dispossession, is indeed He whom Romano Guardini contemplated, this man completely identified with His mission, whose impenetrable experience constitutes, nevertheless, the secret of every Christian life.

Notes*

NOTE TO THE PREFACE

[1] D. Mollat, "Jean l'Evangéliste," DS, vol. 8, cols. 192-247.

NOTES TO CHAPTER 1

[1] Cf. the art. "Esprit Saint," DS, vol. 4, col. 1252.

NOTES TO CHAPTER 2

[1] E. Güttgemans, *Der leidende Apostel und sein Herr. Studien zur paulinischen Christologie* (Göttingen, 1966).

[2] E. Käsemann, *Perspectives of Paul* (Philadelphia, 1971).

[3] See vol. 5 of the present series, *Imitating Christ*, pp. 19-24.

[4] J. Gnilka, *Der Epheserbrief* (Freiburg-im-Breisgau, 1971), pp. 243-245.

NOTES TO CHAPTER 3

[1] See J. Jeremias, *Theologie des Neuen Testaments.* I, *Die Verkündigung Jesu* (Gütersloh, 1971), pp. 61-62.

[2] E. Neuhäusler, *Exigence de Dieu et morale chrétienne.* Lectio divina 70 (Paris, 1971), p. 25.

---

*Since this series is intended for English readers only, many references in the original articles of the DS to publications in foreign languages have been omitted. All titles of primary sources have been translated into their English equivalents. When quotations from secondary sources are given in the body of the text, reference is made in the footnotes to the book or article from which the translation has been made.

Except for the passages from de Grandmaison's *Jesus Christ,* the translator of the present volume has made her own English version of all quotations cited by the author in French.

[3] See J. Jeremias, *The Prayers of Jesus. Studies in Biblical Theology*, 2nd ser., 6 (London-Naperville, Ill., 1967).

[4] D. Flusser, *Jésus* (Paris, 1970), pp. 106-108 and n. 162.

[5] See vol. 5 of the present series, *Imitating Christ*, pp. 10-12.

[6] E. Lohmeyer, *Das Evangelium des Markus* (Göttingen, 1967[17]), p. 242.

[7] J. Jeremias, *Theologie des Neuen Testaments. I, Die Verkündigung Jesu* (Gütersloh, 1971), pp. 61-62.

[8] R. Bultmann, *Die Theologie des Neuen Testaments* (Tübingen, 1968[6]), pp. 29-31.

[9] H. Urs von Balthasar, *La foi du Christ* (Paris, 1968), p. 181.

[10] J. Radermakers, *Au fil de l'Evangile selon saint Matthieu*, II (Heverlee-Louvain, 1972), 345-348.

NOTES TO CHAPTER 4

[1] See the art. "Jean l'Evangéliste," by D. Mollat, DS, vol. 8, cols. 192-247.

[2] C. H. Dodd, "Une parabole cachée dans le quatrième Evangile," *Revue d'histoire et de philosophie religieuse*, 42 (1962), 107-115.

[3] See Mollat, col. 205.

[4] *Ibid.*, especially cols. 225-226.

[5] *Ibid.*, col. 205.

NOTES TO CHAPTER 5

[1] L. de Grandmaison, *Jesus Christ*, tr. Dom Basil Whelan, O.S.B., Ada Lane, and Douglas Carter (New York, 1961), pp. 86, 111-112.

[2] A. von Harnack, *L'essence du Christianisme* (Paris, 1907), pp. 50-52.

[3] M.-J. Lagrange, *L'Evangile de Jésus-Christ* (Paris, 1928), pp. 612-622.

[4] Cited by G. Ebeling, *Théologie et proclamation* (Paris, 1972), p. 174.

[5] R. Marlé, *Bultmann et l'interprétation du Nouveau Testament* (Paris, 1966[2]), p. 179, n. 27.

[6] R. Bultmann, *Foi et compréhension*, II (Paris, 1969), 219.

[7] *Ibid.*, I, 231.

[8] *Ibid.*, II, 57.

[9] *Ibid.*, I, 228-229.

[10] *Ibid.*, II, 399.

[11] *Ibid.*, I, 229.

[12] K. Barth, *Dogmatique*, IV.2.1 (Geneva, 1968), 116.

[13] *Ibid.*, IV.2.1, 203.

[14] *Ibid.*, IV.4 (Geneva, 1972), 90-91.

[15] R. Guardini, *Le Seigneur,* I (Paris, 1946), 7.

[16] *Ibid.*, II, 46-47.

[17] *Ibid.*, II, 50-51.

[18] *Ibid.*, I, 180.

[19] *Ibid.*, I, 7, 181.

[20] *Ibid.*, II, 174.

[21] *Ibid.*, II, 177.

[22] Bultmann, II, 219.

[23] Hans Urs von Balthasar, *La gloire et la croix* (Paris, 1965).

[24] *Ibid.*, I, 273.

[25] *Ibid.*, I, 254.

[26] *Ibid.*, I, 273.

[27] *Ibid.*, I, 276-277 (French translation slightly modified by the author of this study).

[28] *Ibid.*, I, 279.

[29] *Ibid.*, I, 275.

[30] *Ibid.*, I, 276.

BIBLIOGRAPHY

Chapter 1

Bruner, F. D. *A Theology of the Holy Spirit. The Pentecostal Experience and the New Testament Witness.* Grand Rapids: 1970.

Dana, H. E. *The Holy Spirit in Acts.* Kansas City: 1943.

Dibelius, M. *Studies in the Acts of the Apostles,* ed. H. Greeven. New York: 1956.

Haenchen, E. *Acts of the Apostles—A Commentary.* Westminster, Md.: 1971.

Lampe, G. W. H. "The Holy Spirit in the Writings of St. Luke," in *Studies in the Gospels.* In Memory of R. H. Lightfoot, ed. D. E. Nineham. Oxford: 1955.

Munck, J. *The Acts of the Apostles.* The Anchor Bible. Garden City: 1967.

Schweizer, E. *"Pneuma,* etc.," TDNT, VI, 404-415.

Strathmann, H. *"Martus,* etc.," TDNT, IV, 474-514.

Zehnle, R. *Tradition and Lukan Reinterpretation in Peter's Speeches of Acts 2 and 3.* Nashville-New York: 1971.

Chapter 2

Bornkamm, G. *Paul.* New York: 1971.

Bouttier, M. *Christianity according to Paul. Studies in Biblical Theology.* Naperville, Ill.: 1966.

Cerfaux, L. *The Christian in the Theology of Saint Paul.* New York: 1959.

Käsemann, E. *Perspectives of Paul.* Philadelphia: 1971.

Kümmel, W. *The Theology of the New Testament According to Its Major Witnesses: Jesus, Paul, John.* Nashville-New York: 1973.

Martin, R. P. *An Early Christian Confession. Phil 1:5-11 in Recent Interpretation.* London: 1960.

————. *Carmen Christi. Phil 2:5-11 in Recent Interpretation and in the Setting of Early Christian Worship.* Cambridge: 1967.

Schnackenburg, R. *The Gospel according to St. John.* New York-London: 1968. Cf. I, 494-506, on the pre-existence of Christ.

Schweitzer, A. *The Mysticism of Paul the Apostle.* London: 1953.

Taylor, V. *The Person of Christ in New Testament Teaching.* London: 1958.

72

Chapter 3

Barrett, C. K. *Jesus and the Gospel Tradition*. London: 1967.

Benoit, P. *The Passion and Resurrection of Jesus Christ*. New York: 1969.

Bornkamm, G. *Jesus of Nazareth*. London: 1966.

Bultmann, G. *Jesus and the Word*. New York-London: 1934.

———. *Theology of the New Testament*. New York: 1951-1955.

Colpe, C. *"Ho huios tou authropou,"* TDNT, VIII, 400-477.

Cullman, O. *The Christology of the New Testament*. Philadelphia: 1959.

———. *Peter, Disciple, Apostle, Martyr. A Historical and Theological Study*. London-Philadelphia: 1962².

Dalman, G. *Jesus-Jeshua. Studies in the Gospels*. New York: 1929.

Davies, W. D. *The Setting of the Sermon on the Mount*. Cambridge: 1964.

Dibelius, M. *Jesus*. Philadelphia: 1949.

Dodd, C. H. *The Founder of Christianity*. London: 1971.

Flusser, D. *Jesus*. New York: 1969.

Goguel, M. *The Life of Jesus*. New York: 1933; London: 1958. Also translated as *Jesus and the Origins of Christianity*, Vol. 1. New York: 1960.

Grandmaison, L. de. *Jesus Christ*. New York: 1961.

Guillet, J. *The Consciousness of Jesus.* New York: 1972.

Hahn, F. *The Titles of Jesus in Christology—Their History in Early Christianity*. Cleveland-London: 1969.

Jeremias, J. *The Eucharistic Words of Jesus*. New York: 1966³.

———. *New Testament Theology*. Vol. 1, *The Proclamation of Jesus*. London-New York: 1971.

———. *The Prayers of Jesus. Studies in Biblical Theology*. London-Naperville, Ill.: 1967.

———. *The Problem of the Historical Jesus*. Philadelphia: 1964.

Klausner, J. *Jesus of Nazareth—His Life, Times, and Teaching*. New York: 1925.

Lagrange, M. J. *The Gospel of Jesus Christ*. London: 1938; Westminster, Md.: 1967.

Lebreton, J. *The Life and Teaching of Jesus Christ*. London: 1957.

Leon-Dufour, X. *The Gospels and the Jesus of History*. London-New York: 1968.

Loos, H. van der. *The Miracles of Jesus*. Leiden: 1965.

Manson, T. W. *Jesus the Messiah*. London: 1943.

———. *The Sayings of Jesus*. London: 1949.

————. *The Servant-Messiah. A Study of the Public Ministry of Jesus.* Cambridge: 1953.

Marxsen, W. *The Beginning of Christology: A Study in Its Problems.* Philadelphia: 1969.

————. *The Lord's Supper as a Christological Problem.* Philadelphia: 1970.

Pannenberg, W. *Jesus: God and Man.* Philadelphia-London: 1968.

Perrin, N. *The Kingdom of God in the Teaching of Jesus.* London: 1963.

Robinson, J. M. *A New Quest of the Historical Jesus.* Naperville, Ill.-London: 1959.

Sanders, J. T. *The New Testament Christological Hymns—Their Historical Background.* London: 1971.

Schnackenburg, R. *God's Rule and Kingdom.* New York: 1963.

Schweitzer, A. *The Quest of the Historical Jesus.* New York: 1968.

Schweizer, E. *Jesus.* Richmond, Va.-London: 1971.

Stauffer, E. *Jesus and His Story.* New York: 1960; London: 1960.

Taylor, V. *The Life and Ministry of Jesus.* London: 1954.

————. *The Person of Christ in New Testament Teaching.* London: 1958.

Chapter 4

The bibliography is indicated in D. Mollat, "Jean l'Evangéliste," DS, vol. 8, cols. 192-247.

Chapter 5

Barth, K. *Church Dogmatics.* New York-Edinburgh: 1955—.

Bultmann, R. *Essays Philosophical and Theological.* London-New York: 1955.

————. *Existence and Faith.* New York: 1960.

————. *Faith and Understanding,* ed. with an Introduction by R. W. Funk. New York: 1969.

Ebeling, G. *Theology and Proclamation. Dialogue with Bultmann.* Philadelphia: 1966.

Grandmaison, L. de. *Jesus Christ.* New York: 1961.

Guardini, R. *The Lord.* Chicago: 1954.

Harnack, A. von. *What Is Christianity?* (Harper Torchbacks) New York: 1957.

Lagrange, M.-J. *The Gospel of Jesus Christ.* London: 1938; Westminster, Md.: 1967.

Marlé, R. *Bultmann and Christian Faith.* Westminster, Md.: 1967.